Twayne's United States Authors Series

Sylvia E. Bowman, *Editor*

INDIANA UNIVERSITY

Carl Sandburg

CARL SANDBURG

by **RICHARD CROWDER**

Purdue University

 47

Twayne Publishers, Inc. ::   New York

MANUFACTURED IN THE UNITED STATES OF AMERICA BY
UNITED PRINTING SERVICES, INC.
NEW HAVEN, CONN.

Preface

ON A STAGE before a rapt audience, as he twangs away at four or five chords on a guitar and sings with an Illinois nasality, Carl Sandburg is helping to preserve the art of the American people. He may have explained to his hearers that the ribald song he is singing was known in southern Indiana in the 1820's, that surely Abraham Lincoln had sung it with his neighbors. He may or may not have explained that the words are to be found in *The American Songbag*, a scholarly collection of folk songs of all categories. It is not as a scholar that Sandburg wants to be received; yet scholarly fascination with the folklore and folkways of America from the early nineteenth century to the middle of the twentieth has led him to investigate and record his materials as thoroughly as any professor stealing time from paper-grading and classroom teaching.

Maintaining a studied unkemptness of dress and a carefully shaggy head of hair, Sandburg has built an image of himself as one of the common people—tall, broad, rough-hewn, deep-voiced. At the same time, he has wanted to be their spokesman. He has created, as their representative, a definite literary personality, skillful, worldly, conscious of what he is doing—at times simple and direct, at times rhapsodic, sometimes obscure. (He himself admits that he has forgotten the meaning of poems written long ago.)

Sandburg's reputation as a folk singer is only one side of his popular appeal. His audiences know him as the author of a staggeringly detailed biography of America's greatest folk hero, Abraham Lincoln, and as a writer who dared to open a poem with the cacophonous line "Hog Butcher for the World." They may or may not be aware that he rocked the literary world with "Chicago" in 1914, when verse was beginning to revitalize itself after decades of dreary prettiness and shallow melancholy. They may or may not know that *Abraham Lincoln* is not his only essay into biography and that he is also a novelist and a writer of children's books.

This *persona* as mouthpiece of the common man has been a natural development. Though artful and aware, Sandburg has not had to force his point of view. Rather, his work and life have been all of a piece. Wallace Stevens represented another kind of integrity. At least on the surface he lived one kind of life as an insurance executive and another as a poet, and was honest in both. Sandburg, on the other hand, not only was long in immediate contact with the laboring classes but has been almost exclusively motivated by workers and his Populist experience. He found his point of view in his boyhood and has never deviated from it. If in one way such a position appears static, in another way it ought not to be so deprecated. Though he has had no "periods" and no perceptive intellectual maturation since his first public statement in *Poetry: A Magazine of Verse* a half century ago, he has managed to keep his few issues quite alive through various means and thus to remain prominent on the stage of twentieth-century American letters. Many serious connoisseurs of poetry do not find him interesting any more, but he does still have an appeal for less rarefied readers. He does not deserve to be lost.

His attitude, then, is not a mere mask, nor is it the result of intellectual exercise leading to the reception of a formal philosophic system. It is, rather, the flowering from the roots of his beginning. So indivisible are his work and life that this book makes no attempt to separate them. Biography and literary analysis here move side by side.

In reviewing the six volumes of Sandburg's life of Lincoln, historians said that they could not call the work history, for the author had added little, if any, information and indeed virtually no insights to what had already found statement. They were of the opinion, rather, that this biography had been the loving labor of a poet: what had given it value and interest was the way he had stated the familiar facts and opinions as well as the unmistakable emotional vigor which he had poured into his work.

Much the same comment might be made about Sandburg's other principal prose books. His novel, *Remembrance Rock,* is not a good novel; but it is a testimony—often to the point of tedium—of patriotic affirmation and fervor. *Always the Young Strangers* is autobiographical in substance, but in effect it is

close to his poetry—to *Good Morning, America*, for example—
evoking a mood, the details of the narrative being nothing extra-
ordinary. For this reason it is better to consider all the books as
coming from the pen of a poet and to see what they show of
the talent of that poet—a maker, a user of words and of structure
to convey meaning sometimes beyond meaning.

This study gives only a passing glance at those books of Carl
Sandburg that cannot be classified as literature in the sense of
belles-lettres. The others are treated at greater length: *Chicago
Poems; Cornhuskers; Smoke and Steel; Slabs of the Sunburnt
West; Good Morning, America;* and *The People, Yes;* the six
volumes of the life of Lincoln: *Abraham Lincoln: The Prairie
Years* and *Abraham Lincoln: The War Years;* the autobiographi-
cal *Always the Young Strangers;* and the novel, *Remembrance
Rock.*

The Chicago Race Riots and *Home Front Memo* are chiefly
collections of newspaper items. The various *Rootabaga* books
and *Potato Face* are fantasies of interest to children. *The American Songbag* and *The New American Songbag* are repositories
of folk music. *Steichen the Photographer* is a brief introduction
to a collection of photographs. *A Lincoln and Whitman Miscellany, Mary Lincoln, Wife and Widow,* and *Lincoln Collector:
the Story of Oliver R. Barrett's Great Private Collection* are of
historical but not of literary interest. Sandburg's popularity has
led to still other books made up of selections from his earlier
work (sometimes with minor additions and corrections) and to
numerous reprints. The concern in this book is with the ten
major works: the book describing his first twenty years, the six
books of verse, the six volumes of his life of Lincoln (two titles),
and his novel.

The object of this present book is five-fold: (1) to give the
details of Sandburg's life that are relevant to his writing; (2)
to summarize the prose and sample the verse content of his
books; (3) to review the critics' reception of each major work;
(4) to analyze the themes and the craftsmanship in each volume; and (5) to appraise Sandburg's achievement; that is, to
determine, in so far as is possible with an author who is still
publishing, his permanent position in American letters.

In making acknowledgments, I must admit to a free-wheel-
ing pirating of ideas, interpretations, and probably even phrases

from the scores of reviews and critical articles available about Sandburg. 1 have leaned heavily on the books by Karl W. Detzer and Harry Golden for details of the life. Heads of libraries and their patient staffs have been unfailingly kind. Particularly must I recognize Professor John H. Moriarty, Director of the Purdue University libraries; Professor Warren Morris, head librarian at Knox College; and Dean Robert Downs of the University of Illinois libraries. Professor Sylvia E. Bowman has been an expert and sympathetic editor.

—RICHARD CROWDER

Purdue University

Acknowledgments

Harcourt, Brace and World, Inc., has granted the following permissions to reprint from copyrighted material:

From *Smoke and Steel* by Carl Sandburg. Copyright 1920 by Harcourt, Brace and World, Inc. Copyright renewed 1948 by Carl Sandburg.

From *Slabs of the Sunburnt West* by Carl Sandburg. Copyright 1922 by Harcourt, Brace and World, Inc. Copyright renewed 1950 by Carl Sandburg.

From *Abraham Lincoln: The Prairie Years* by Carl Sandburg. Copyright 1926 by Harcourt, Brace and World, Inc. Copyright renewed 1954 by Carl Sandburg.

From *Selected Poems* (Rebecca West, ed.) by Carl Sandburg. Copyright 1926 by Harcourt, Brace and World, Inc. Copyright renewed 1954 by Carl Sandburg.

From *Good Morning, America* by Carl Sandburg. Copyright 1928 by Harcourt, Brace and World, Inc. Copyright renewed 1956 by Carl Sandburg.

From *Steichen the Photographer* by Carl Sandburg. Copyright 1929 by Harcourt, Brace and World, Inc. Copyright renewed 1957 by Carl Sandburg.

From *The People, Yes* by Carl Sandburg. Copyright 1936 by Harcourt, Brace and World, Inc.

From *Abraham Lincoln: The War Years* by Carl Sandburg. Copyright 1939 by Harcourt, Brace and World, Inc.

From *Remembrance Rock* by Carl Sandburg. Copyright 1948 by Harcourt, Brace and World, Inc.

From *Always the Young Strangers* by Carl Sandburg. Copyright 1952, 1953 by Carl Sandburg.

Permissions from other sources are as follows:

"June" and random lines. From *Chicago Poems* by Carl Sandburg. Copyright 1916 by Holt, Rinehart and Winston, Inc. Copyright renewed 1944 by Carl Sandburg. Reprinted by permission of Holt, Rinehart and Winston, Inc.

Contents

Chronology

1878   Carl Sandburg born January 6, Galesburg, Illinois, son of August and Clara.
1891   Left school after eighth grade to work at odd jobs.
1894   First visit to Chicago.
1897   Worked in Iowa, Kansas, Nebraska, Colorado.
1898   Apprenticed to housepainter in Galesburg. Enlisted in Sixth Illinois Regiment. Served in Puerto Rico during war with Spain. Returned to Galesburg. Enrolled as special student in Lombard College.
1899   Appointed to West Point. Stayed two weeks in summer. Returned to Lombard.
1902   Without graduating, left Lombard to wander over country.
1904   Returned to Galesburg. Philip Green Wright, his favorite professor, published Sandburg's *In Reckless Ecstasy, The Plaint of a Rose, Incidentals* on the Asgard Press.
1906   Left Galesburg permanently.
1907- Associate editor of *The Lyceumite*, Chicago.
1908
1908   In Wisconsin as district organizer for Social-Democratic party. June 15 married Lillian ("Paula") Steichen. Set up housekeeping in Appleton.
1909   Moved to Milwaukee. Reporter for *Journal* and other newspapers.
1910- Private secretary to Emil Seidel, mayor of Milwaukee.
1912
1910   Father died. *Joseffy: An Appreciation.*
1911   Birth of Margaret.
1912   Moved to Chicago. Joined *World* staff briefly; went over to *Day Book.*
1913   On staff of *System* several months. Returned to *Day Book.*
1914   Nine "Chicago Poems" in *Poetry: A Magazine of Verse.* Won Helen Haire Levinson Prize for best poems of the year. Birth of Janet. Moved to suburban Maywood.
1916   *Chicago Poems.*
1917   *Day Book* closed down. Eventually joined *Daily News.*

1918 To Stockholm for Newspaper Enterprise Association. *Cornhuskers.*

1919 Returned to *Daily News.* Appointed motion-picture editor. Shared Poetry Society of America Prize. *The Chicago Race Riots.* Moved family to Elmhurst.

1920 First platform performance at a college—Cornell College, Mount Vernon, Iowa. *Smoke and Steel.* Birth of Helga.

1921 Again shared Poetry Society of America Prize.

1922 *Slabs of the Sunburnt West. Rootabaga Stories.*

1923 *Rootabaga Pigeons.*

1926 *Abraham Lincoln: The Prairie Years.* Bought house at Harbert, Michigan, as summer residence. *Selected Poems,* Rebecca West, editor, published in London. Mother died.

1927 *The American Songbag.*

1928 Phi Beta Kappa poet at Harvard. Litt. D., Lombard. *Good Morning, America.*

1929 Litt. D., Knox. *Steichen the Photographer.*

1930 *Potato Face. Early Moon.*

1931 Litt. D., Northwestern.

1932 Left *Daily News.* Settled at Harbert. *Mary Lincoln, Wife and Widow.*

1934 Lecturer, University of Hawaii.

1936 *The People, Yes.*

1939 *Abraham Lincoln: The War Years.*

1940 Pulitzer Prize for history. Elected to American Academy of Arts and Letters. Special diploma, Lincoln Memorial University, Mount Harrogate, Tennessee. Litt. D., Lafayette, Wesleyan, Yale, Harvard. Six lectures, Walgreen Fund, University of Chicago.

1941 Litt. D., Syracuse, Dartmouth. LL.D., Rollins.

1942- During World War II, wrote weekly column for Chicago
1945 *Times* Syndicate; narrator for "Cavalcade of America" and other radio programs; wrote commentary for U. S. Government film *Bomber;* made foreign broadcasts for Office of War Information.

1942 Wrote captions for *Road to Victory,* Museum of Modern Art, New York. *Storm over the Land.*

1943 Phi Beta Kappa poet at William and Mary. *Home Front Memo.*

1945 Moved to Connemara, Flat Rock, North Carolina.

1946 Dedication of birthplace at Galesburg.
1948 LL.D., Augustana. *Remembrance Rock.*
1950 Ph.D. (honorary), Uppsala (Sweden). *Complete Poems.* Pulitzer Prize for poetry. *The New American Songbag.*
1952 American Academy of Arts and Letters gold medal for history and biography.
1953 *Always the Young Strangers.* "Carl Sandburg Day" in Chicago, January 6. Received Commanders Cup of the Order of the Northern Star (Sweden). Poetry Society of America gold medal. Tamiment Institute award. LL.D., Illinois.
1954 New York Civil War Round Table silver medal. *Abraham Lincoln: The Prairie Years and the War Years* (one volume).
1955 Boston Arts Festival poetry prize. Litt. D., North Carolina. Award of Merit, University of Louisville. *Prairie-Town Boy.*
1956 University of Illinois paid $50,000 for four tons of Sandburg's books, letters, manuscripts, and other papers. Humanities award, Albert Einstein College of Medicine, New York.
1957 *The Sandburg Range.*
1958 Supported the release of Nathan Leopold and of Ezra Pound. Made "Honorary Ambassador" of North Carolina on "Sandburg Day."
1959 Lincoln Day address, February 12, in Washington before both Houses of Congress, Supreme Court members, Eisenhower cabinet, diplomatic corps. Litt. D., Upsala College (New Jersey). Honored in Stockholm at Swedish-American Day. Received "Litteris et Artibus" medal from King Gustav VI.
1960 Went to Hollywood as consultant for film of life of Christ, *The Greatest Story Ever Told. Harvest Poems. Wind Song.*
1961 With Robert Frost and Archibald MacLeish, asked to write creed for proposed National Cultural Center in Washington.
1962 Member National Committee for Support of the Public Schools. Designated "poet laureate of Illinois."
1963 *Honey and Salt.*

Carl Sandburg

CHAPTER 1

A Young Stranger

I *The Son of Immigrants*

CARL SANDBURG was seventy-five years old on January 6, 1953.[1] On this day Harcourt, Brace and Company published his account of the first twenty years of his life, *Always the Young Strangers*. He had earned the right to make public his recollections, for he had achieved renown as poet, as biographer, as journalist, as platform artist. But he did not think of this new book as an autobiography so much as an account of "the life of a town and a community, something of the life of the nation. If it should be called anything, it is the biography of a town filtered through the life of a boy."[2] The title derived from a poem he had written over thirty years before called "Broken-Face Gargoyles":

> ... the young strangers, coming, coming, always coming.
>
> It is early.
> I shall yet be footloose.[3]

The hope of America, the foundation of her dream, was these new generations, meeting new crises, always surmounting the difficulties of history. As he recalled his youth, Sandburg felt he had been sharing the destiny of these "young strangers."

Galesburg, Illinois, was a prairie town settled a generation before Carl's birth by New Englanders, who had established those symbols of culture, churches and colleges, even before the railroads had reached the community. They had brought civilization with them. Then, when the Chicago, Burlington, and Quincy Railroad (the "Q") built shops in the town and the Santa Fe made it a stop on its way to and from Chicago, thousands of

Irish Catholics and Swedish Lutherans were attracted by the opportunities for jobs.

August Sandburg was a steady man of peasant origin who went faithfully to his job in the yards of the "Q" day after day, year in and year out. Though he never learned to write and was forced to sign documents with an "X," he did so with solemn dignity. He could read Swedish, however, and devoured his Bible, for he was devout if not always regular in church attendance. A stern man, he nevertheless loved his wife and children even though his show of affection was not effusive. His wage—fourteen cents an hour—was meager enough, but since his wife Clara was a frugal housekeeper and mother, he was able to save money.

Clara was of different temperament from her husband. Patient, gentle, and more demonstrative in her love, she was able to give to her children the tender attention that filled any gap her husband's diffidence might have left. She also complemented August in being able to read and write in both Swedish and English. She could help and encourage her children in their schooling.

The Sandburg's first son, their second child, was born shortly after midnight on January 6, 1878. As soon as was feasible, he was baptized Carl August. A second son arrived less than two years later. Their first house, where Carl was born, was much too small—three tiny rooms near the tracks of the "Q." Before Carl was five, the family had moved twice and at last settled in more commodious quarters on Berrien Street. This double house was large enough to accommodate the present family and the children who were almost sure to come.

Soon after young Carl started in grade school, he began signing himself "Charles A. Sandburg," thinking this to be a more American name than he had been christened with. His father always had difficulty with the pronunciation, however, and had to resort to "Sharley." His brothers and sisters and then his schoolmates called him "Cully," a nickname that stayed with him through college.

August went quietly along in his job, earning at best nine dollars a week, out of which came food costs and payments on the house. Not a joiner, August refused to have anything to do with the strike of the railroad engineers in 1888. He was a

Lutheran and a Republican, and these were affiliations enough for him. Moreover, why should he jeopardize his job by aligning himself with firebrands and mavericks?

With his income less than two dollars a day and with his family growing, August could not afford to send "Sharley" to high school. Hence, at the age of thirteen, the boy went to work after eight grades of schooling. For six years he performed an astonishing variety of odd jobs about the town. He delivered milk; he helped to cut ice; he sold oranges and bananas on street corners; he helped shift scenery for traveling shows at the opera house; he labored on nearby farms. Apparently he was willing to try anything. In later years he thought the most important job he ever had in the town was shining shoes and sweeping the floor at Humphrey's barbershop. Here he could listen to men of all sorts and conditions exchange opinions, philosophize, argue over politics and religion, and tell stories about the past of the town and of the state of Illinois. He began to be engrossed by the idiom of the Midwest: these men may have talked in worn, familiar phrases, but the words were made meaningful by emotion and by the depths of comradeship. Everyday people simply do not talk brilliantly; they carry on the work of the community and express their feelings in the platitudes that they have, inherited from generations before.

> If your right foot itches you will soon start on a journey, if it's your left foot you will go where you are not wanted.
>
> .   .   .   .
>
> Lightning in the north means rain, lightning in the south means dry weather.
>
> *(CP*, 514-15)

Following the pattern of other Swedish families, the Sandburgs saw to it that Cully was confirmed at the age of thirteen (about the time he left school), but he never became a member of the Swedish-Lutheran Church—or of any church. He later came to the opinion that every belief in a Creator has elements to recommend it, but he himself preferred to attach his allegiance to causes other than formal religion.

He had been out of school two years when Governor Altgeld granted pardon to the four survivors of the controversial Chicago Haymarket riots. The boy recollected the day, six years before, when the other prisoners had been executed. At fifteen now he became an admirer of Altgeld, a man of tremendous courage, possessed of a keen sense of justice for the underdog— the immigrant and the common laborer. Cully was beginning to think in terms of the plain people, to identify himself consciously with them.

When at the age of sixteen he heard the glittering oratory of William Jennings Bryan, he announced that he would thence-forth be a Democrat—much to the chagrin of his hard-working but right-wing father. Although Cully finally recognized that Bryan's glitter did not house much gold, the boy's conversion to the Democrats was more or less permanent.

That same year, in June, he had his first view of a large city, the place he was to celebrate in later years, Chicago, the Windy City. As a railroad man, August was able to secure a pass on the C. B. & Q. so that his son could see the sights. With only a little cash, he had to eat very cheap food, but he absorbed the spectacle of urban bustle, his steady, deep eyes missing nothing, including the vast and tragic contrast between the rich and the poor and between the congestion of the slums and the freedom of Lake Michigan.

> I came sudden, at the city's edge,
> On a blue burst of lake,
> Long lake waves breaking under the sun
> On a spray-flung curve of shore. ᴗ . .
> (*CP*, 5)

Though he was not to return to Chicago for years, his first impressions formed a solid base for his later point of view.

On October 7, 1896, Galesburg celebrated the fortieth anniversary of the Lincoln-Douglas debate at Knox College. The boy was able to get away from his work to attend the program. On the platform he saw men of influence, men who had known Lincoln. The president of the New York Central Railroad, Chauncey M. Depew, had helped re-elect Lincoln in New York State in 1864. The Civil War President's own ·son was there—Robert Todd Lincoln. It occurred to young Sandburg to wonder what Robert and his father had talked about. The Galesburg boy felt that the son had strayed from the father's tradition when, as a lawyer for the Pullman Company, he had been on the side of management in the labor strike of 1894. Youthful though he was, Cully's sympathies were fairly well lined up by this time.

In the summer of 1897—he was now well past his nineteenth birthday—he grew restless. He had seen Chicago; he wanted to see more of the United States. So he took off for the West, riding in a box car to Fort Madison, Iowa, thence down to Keokuk. He had crossed the Mississippi for the first time. At Keokuk he tried a job as a lunch-counter waiter but stayed only one day, his boss giving ample evidence of being an irresponsible drunkard. Without asking for his pay, Cully moved on to Bean Lake in Missouri, where for ten days he was a member of a railroad section gang; but again, this time unable to digest a monotonous diet of fried potatoes and pork, he set out before collecting his wages. For some weeks he went from job to job, selling hot tamales in Kansas City, pitching wheat bundles in Pawnee County, Kansas. By early fall he had gone as far west as the Windsor Hotel in Denver, where he washed dishes for a few days. Then he turned back towards Illinois. He had learned a great deal and seen a great variety of people. In two small notebooks he had kept an informal log of his travels and had jotted down addresses of people he met. He had also practiced word exercises in his leisure moments, for he was already fascinated with the possibilities of language.

Once more in Galesburg, he apprenticed himself to a housepainter for whom he worked several weeks—until, in fact, the news of the sinking of the *Maine* in Havana harbor arrived. Then, in February, 1898, he enlisted in Company C, Sixth Illinois Regiment of the State Militia, which was mustered in at Springfield, the state capital. After a few months of drill and indoctrination, the regiment set sail from Charleston, South Carolina, and landed in Guantánamo Bay in Cuba. From there the men were transported to Puerto Rico.

In Sandburg's pack were two books: the *Infantry Drill Regulations* (he learned to like the morale-building that discipline produced) and *The New Webster Dictionary and Complete Vest-Pocket Library.*[4] He might be in a fighting army, but he was not going to divorce himself from the words he had come to enjoy adventuring among. (He presented the dictionary to his grandchildren in 1949.) In the intense heat, fighting off mosquitoes and eating bad food, he managed to write back long letters to the Galesburg *Evening Mail*, describing his experiences and reactions. His regiment was involved in only a few skirmishes, but he had enough of war to know the discomfort, the occasional humor, and the boredom it involved. After the speedy defeat of Spain, Company C returned to Springfield, and Sandburg was discharged.

Home again, with $122 discharge pay in his pocket, he reimbursed his father for a loan and with what was left decided to matriculate at Lombard College, for as a veteran he would be entitled to a year's free tuition. Smaller than Knox, its neighboring college of Congregational persuasion, Lombard was under the supervision of the Universalist Church and hence on a considerably liberal base. Cully Sandburg registered as a special student, since he had not had a high school education. He enrolled in courses in inorganic chemistry, Latin, English, and speech—a curriculum reflecting his predilection for language. In four months he would be twenty-one years old.

II *Sandburg's Autobiography*

Many of the details of these twenty years were included in *Always the Young Strangers,* and there were many more, so many in fact that one cannot see any sense of structure beyond the merely chronological. The book is a quiet one: there is no climax; what excitement there is, is the excitement that would come to any small-town Midwestern boy. The incidents, many of them interesting in themselves, are set down, generally speaking, in the order of their occurrence.

But there is more to it than that. The book had come from the pen of an experienced writer. He knew what he was up to.

Without hint of the man to come, the book, however simple its organization, reveals to the sympathetic reader a sense of growth in curiosity and judgment. The young Sandburg had surely learned something from every experience. The fact that he was now remembering vividly the details of his daily life of sixty and even seventy years before shows not only his capacity for recollection, but also his ability to remember particularly; to recall the special sights and sounds that made his experiences his own, however closely they might resemble those of any prairie-town boy. At the time of publication in 1953, the author commented on the psychological effect of composition: "Writing parts of it was very much fun, indeed. As I went along, things kept coming back out of my boyhood, and by putting them down, I'm released from them. People kept coming back, too. As I would meet them while carrying milk near St. Pat's Church."[5]

Whatever the effect on the author, the book is nevertheless about an education. It cannot be classed with the current, sophisticated studies of initiation, of escape from innocence; but it does tell about the gaining and retaining of knowledge and of transmuting it into wisdom and judgment, though never in pretentious or self-conscious style, but almost invariably in plain statement.

> There was Stella Garrity. Her name was in the papers several times when her house was raided and the men in the patrol wagon tried to hide their faces. She kept a house next west of the Narrow Gauge Railway on Berrien Street. She was a massively constructed woman, with the curves of a burlesque star. In her case I can use her right name. I believe she would prefer to be mentioned rather than have her name omitted. She was a show-off, no other woman of the town quite so flagrant about being seen publicly in dashing fine clothes. . . .
>
> After her place was raided and she was fined several times and men were afraid of being caught in raids on her house, Stella left town . . . (*Strangers*, 338-39).

The reader learns of Sandburg's early discovery of and devotion to music. He learns of the boy's appetite for reading. He sees the birth of interest in politics during the Blaine-Cleveland campaign. Social justice comes to the fore at the time of Governor Altgeld's brave stand concerning the Chicago anarchists.

During his career as odd-jobs man Cully came to know most of the people in the town, from the most respected to the most flagrantly immoral and the laziest, no-account bum. He learned to make distinctions, to formulate value judgments. He learned a good deal about good and evil in the long run. Somehow, he himself never succumbed to the temptations that most assuredly were often in his way. The religious rigors of his upbringing and genuine love of his parents kept him morally sound. In this book he wrote of his parents at considerable length, matter-of-factly but with obvious fondness.

In all the four hundred-odd pages of *Always the Young Strangers* there is only an occasional suggestion of the chanting, raucous, or rhapsodic quality of much of Sandburg's poetry. He here resorted appropriately to the cadences, the words, and the idiom of his boyhood. Though his writing was that of a man, he was artistically successful in conveying the emotions of a boy. As a result, the craftsman's language sometimes breaks down and the uncouth locutions of childhood take over: ". . . He didn't holler it nor make a face at me. He said it kind of soft . . ." (*Strangers,* 283); ". . . Us kids asked in Galesburg . . ." (*Strangers,* 131). But only now and then do the syntactical and grammatical gaucheries of a son of Swedish immigrants burst out. The boy had come to love words and spent many spare hours perusing encyclopedias, *The Youth's Companion,* and books of every description. Through the years—many spent as a newspaper reporter—he achieved an enviable ability to make details clear. If as an old man he was occasionally tedious and circumlocutory, his book as a whole nevertheless added up to a vivid beginning of his life story.

The grown man so rarely intrudes that it could not have been Sandburg's purpose to reveal the psychological causes, the specific instances, the traumata that may have influenced his adult personality; for, in the telling, there are no points of focus, no discrimination, just detail piled on detail. But there is always the large design, the chronological ordering, set forth with simple directness and with the determined facing away from compromise that characterized the whole of Sandburg's rearing. If in succession the incidents lack drama, still they show the building of character, the forming of personality.

His sentences sometimes have the bluntness of a second language. (He had actually learned Swedish words first, though this fact is only incidental.) In spite of the grammatical "blunders," however, this trait cannot be labeled as affected; it is, rather, boyhood bursting through. The style is one of simple realism without decoration. Sandburg is trying to support no thesis, impress no *littérateur.* The language is closer to the language of ordinary speech than to the finesses of the dilettante's pen. He makes no point of style, but shares the experience or person or thing he is describing with clarity, with no show of virtuosity.

Though Sandburg claimed not to have had any connection with the Imagists, many of his early poems came from a head and heart that subscribed to an identical creed. In this book, written long after the Imagist vogue, one sees the influence of that emphasis on single-minded clarity. He makes virtually no effort to comment; he simply states flatly what he has to say and lets it go at that. If his poetry of the 1930's is befogged in a shapeless philosophy of proletarianism without a plan, with occasional distorted syntax, with imagery sometimes uncontrolled and uncontrolling, such weaknesses are not to be found in *Always the Young Strangers*. Subject matter is now unquestionably in control. Modest as it is, the material keeps the style from overflowing into involved and florid periods; it keeps the writer from overreaching himself as he had done in his poems from time to time.

The success of this book rests in the balance Sandburg maintained between the Swedish immigrant's son that he had been and the American poet and historian that he had become. He had got back to the boy who was not yet a poet, but he had maintained sufficient distance to see him as he was and not sentimentally as he might wish him to have been. The result is an authentic condensation of the American Dream, Sandburg's constant theme. By telling his very own story with simplicity and with the intensity of a pared-down style, he has given his reader a history not only of himself but of his place and time.

Many readers of *Always the Young Strangers* can identify with him. In that respect he achieves universality. The Midwest has produced thousands of men and women who lived, like Sandburg, a close-knit family life with warmth and simple dignity; and they, as they read, must have felt a similar emotional satisfaction from well-spent days unmarred by bitterness or by compulsively driving ambition. This is not to say that Sandburg was content to drift, for he did "revolt" from his fairly aimless teen-age existence; but he had come from a home of love and had felt no necessity to kick and gouge in order to "get ahead."

Indeed, the book is marked by an abundance of love. The dynamics change from time to time: it is now wistful, now hearty and robust. It is, however, full of affection and warmth.

Not only does the author show a love for people, but he demonstrates an intense love for his country (no 1920's expatriate he) and for the land, the earth from which must come man's sustenance. In analysis, the details of the boy's life were often harsh, even cruel. They would have turned a boy of another nature and another background into a cynic, if not an out-and-out revolutionary. But Cully had taken no exception to the vicissitudes of his experience. He managed to find goodness everywhere. What was evil did not corrupt him. What he could not help he simply observed, and let alone.

Though the chapters are made of the stuff of nostalgia, though the tone is in general mellow, one cannot say that they are in the least sentimental. Filled as the pages are with humanity, Sandburg shows a genuine affection for his kind. He indulges in no self-pity for the hardships he endured. He assumes no bias, contrives no condescension. He works only at achieving his main objective: seemingly artless reporting, frank, honest, dispassionate.

The question might arise as to whether the book is affecting in itself or whether the reader is interested in the haphazard education it records only because of the man he knows it produced beyond the limits of this narrative. The answer must be that *Always the Young Strangers* is a good book. The story of Sandburg's first twenty undistinguished years is told with the wonder we say a poet must have and with the authentic feelings of a boy. These give the details a universality that needs no sequel, no knowledge of fame to come. The mood, for one thing, is constantly buoyant and happy. The reader is absorbed in the boy's experiences because of the humor, the wisdom, and the enduring love of America of an elderly writer with charm, modesty, and passion.

III *College Life*

Always the Young Strangers ends as Cully Sandburg enrolls at Lombard College. In May, 1899, toward the end of his first-year classes, two representatives of the company that he had served with in Puerto Rico the year before came to the Sandburg house to call. Company C, they announced, was entitled to the appointment of a cadet at West Point, and the choice had been narrowed down to Charles A. Sandburg. The news was a surprise. Cully agreed to give the examinations a try. He passed the physical tests hands down, but his omission of high school stood in his way academically: West Pointers had to have knowledge of algebra and geometry. He failed the written examinations. (More successful in that ordeal were Douglas A. MacArthur and Ulysses S. Grant III.) Cully returned quietly to Galesburg and re-entered Lombard in September as a sophomore.

He participated wholeheartedly in the life of the college. In that second year he was business manager of *The Lombard Review, A Live College Journal.* He captained the basketball team, apparently for all four of his college years. He sang with the glee club; he joined the Erosophian Society and debated with right good will, though at first he sometimes failed in trying to think on his feet. In the early spring of 1901, his junior year, he won the Swan Contest (fifteen dollars in gold) with an oration on Ruskin, which *The Lombard Review* published under the title of "A Man with Ideals." He was co-editor of *The Cannibal: Jubilee Year Book* in 1901, and finally in his senior year, he was editor-in-chief of *The Lombard Review.*

To support himself in all this vigorous extracurricular activity, he worked at various jobs on the campus and in the town. He sold stereoscopic views for Underwood and Underwood to the farmers around Galesburg. He was employed by the college as janitor of the gymnasium. He earned some money ringing the college bell to announce the beginning and end of class periods. In the bell tower, incidentally, was stowed an overflow of Universalist tracts and books which he read thoroughly; in fact, he became an authority on arguments for universal salvation. For eight months he served as a fireman for the town of Galesburg at ten dollars a month. He slept in the firehouse and had to leave classes to answer calls.

In June of 1901 he had to undergo an operation for the removal of an unusual film from his eyes. For ten days he lay in utter darkness. The operation was a success, however; for, when at length the bandages were removed, it was only a few weeks before his vision was again clear, and he was able to take his last year at Lombard.

Without doubt his favorite professor was Philip Green Wright, who with commendable versatility taught economics, mathematics, and astronomy as well as English. Recognizing in Cully Sandburg an assiduous and versatile student of unusual ability, he invited him and two others to meet at his house on Sunday afternoons to read and discuss what they had composed during the week. They called themselves The Poor Writers Club. In addition to criticizing their own efforts, they read aloud from Kipling, Turgenev, Mark Twain, and other authors in whom they were currently interested. At one point, Wright and young Sandburg read and thoroughly examined *Das Kapital;* for, as an economist in a liberal college like Lombard, Wright was naturally interested in all points of view.

Governor Altgeld, William Jennings Bryan, the Democratic Party, a visit to Chicago, labor crews in Missouri and Kansas, and now *Das Kapital*—Cully Sandburg's view of life was taking definite shape. Among the pervading influences of the time was the People's Party (the "Populists"), which had its origin in Cincinnati in 1891 and completely fizzled out in the 1904 election. [6] During the 1890's, however, it had represented what Sandburg was beginning to realize he stood for. Its orators lashed out against wars of aggression, capitalistic monopolies, increasing industrialism, the influx of cheap labor from Europe, urban life, and culture resulting from an unearned leisure. Conversely, they advocated an increase in the currency, free coinage of silver, public ownership and operation of railroads, institution of a tax on income, and a limitation on ownership of land. The People's Party had ample grounds for criticism, but in the long run offered little to appeal to a strong-backed young country in no mood for economic controls. Even an underpaid laboring man like August Sandburg would turn a deaf ear toward arguments which sounded dangerously close to revolution.

Some of these ideas, however, struck August's son as sound— especially the anti-war plank, the restlessness with capitalism in its greediest manifestations, and the minimizing of white-collar work. He sympathized with the underprivileged immigrants, though his own immigrant parents had been able to get along on low wages from the "Q." Cully was beginning to see, however, that the metropolis was a necessary and in some ways a stimulating part of a growing civilization, and he began to assent to the concept of a machine age, howbeit with some bewilderment, for the machine was ironically both necessary and degrading.

IV *An Embryo Writer*

Cully Sandburg had entered Lombard College as a provisional student four years before. He had been a good member of the college community, in class work, in sports, in extracurricular literary activity. He had proved himself worthy of a bachelor of arts degree. The *Wanderlust* struck again, though, in the spring of 1902. Making no explanation, he left the campus of his alma mater without his diploma. A mystery to his family and friends, he took to the road, went this time to the East Coast—to New York, New Jersey, Delaware. He continued to sell stereoscopic slides; he rode with hoboes; for six weeks he was a police reporter for the old New York *Daily News*.

One day in 1904 he received in Philadelphia a letter from one of his friends describing the beauties of Wisconsin. With nothing to lose, he began the ride back to the Midwest on a freight train in company with some professional hoboes. He had associated with hoboes before, when as a restless, late teen-ager he had ridden the rods to the West and had worked in the wheat fields of Kansas. Hobo wisdom—whether in aphorism or in anecdote—hobo songs, and hobo language he absorbed with curiosity, almost with passion. But in 1897 he had felt that he was learning about life; now in 1904, at age twenty-six with four years of college education behind him, he added to his emotional experience the appetite of an intellect honed on wide reading, constant writing, and heated discussion; and he was moved too by the rising ambitions that were to lead him into a career as writer. This was the language and the lore of the common people of America, the low strata who had never been adequately represented in their country's literature.

At McKee's Rocks in Pennsylvania he and several of his companions were arrested for riding illegally on the railroad—that is, without tickets. In lieu of a fine, Sandburg spent ten days in the Allegheny County jail in Pittsburgh.

> I got ten days even though I was a veteran of the Spanish-American war.

> Cooped in the same cell with me was an old man, a bricklayer
>   and a booze-fighter.
> But it just happened he, too, was a veteran soldier, and he had
>   fought to preserve the Union and free the niggers (*CP*, 70).

When he wrote about it, he did not turn to recrimination. He made a flat statement; the irony was in the described situation, not in any overt comment.

Late in 1904 he turned once more toward home, more worldly, wiser, but still misunderstood by his fellow townsmen and his hard-working, cautious family. For eight more months he was in the employ of the town as a fireman. He also continued to sell the Underwood and Underwood views to the people of the surrounding countryside. Furthermore, he saw a great deal of his mentor, Professor Wright, who had a hand press (The Asgard Press) in the basement of his house and who turned out modest pamphlets of his own work and that of his acquaintances.

In October, Wright published fifty copies of a pamphlet called *In Reckless Ecstasy* by Charles A. Sandburg. Its thirty-nine pages contained "endeavors at self-expression." Wright's foreword stated that his protégé "reads everything, Boccaccio, Walt Whitman, Emerson, Tolstoi. . . . But literature, even at its best, is but a palled reflection of life; he prefers impressions at first hand. . . ." It is evident that from the beginning Sandburg was a non-intellectual in his writing, if by intellectual one means bookish, eclectic, or as thoroughly indebted to predecessors as are Ezra Pound and T. S. Eliot. Instead, through the years Sandburg was to record what he saw in the light of what he felt; and, if direct description was inadequate for expression of his ultimate idea, he would release a rare symbol or metaphor, which one can suppose would correspond to "reckless ecstasies." (He had derived the title phrase from Marie Corelli.) In fact, in the first sketch the author explained, "I try to express myself sensibly, but if that fails, I will use the reckless ecstasy."

He was formulating the tenets which were to guide him throughout his life as a writer: "I glory in this world of men and women, torn with troubles and lost in sorrow, yet living on to love and laugh and play through it all. My eyes range with pleasure over flowers, prairies, woods, grass, and running water,

and the sea, and the sky and the clouds." In these pages were his
two chief interests: the poor and the oppressed, who always
come up smiling; and nature, whose beauties are always refreshment to the soul.

The Asgard Press also published at this time two other items
by the professor's aspiring friend. One was a ten-page essay
called *The Plaint of a Rose*, a sentimental account of a badly
nourished flower in the shadow of a vigorously beautiful one.
The cover was decorated with hand-painted roses. The other,
a booklet of thirty-two pages, was called, modestly enough,
Incidentals. It contained no verses, but some prose of promising
strength, a set of very short pieces on such topics as "The Pursuit
of Happiness," "Failure," and "What Is a Gentleman?" The
author admitted in the "Apologia" that he might "some day
look back on these incidentals as youthful impertinences." He
saw, too, how difficult it was to express his feelings and describe
his experiences with any satisfying degree of accuracy: "Life is
more vast and strange than anything written about it—words
are only incidentals."

Furthermore, his life as handyman about Galesburg, as a common laborer, and as a police reporter had matured him. "The
hopes of youth have been scorched and scarred in me, but the
romance of life has not burnt out nor the glory of living been
extinguished. I may keep this boy heart of mine, with tears for
the tragic, love for the beautiful, laughter at folly, and silent,
reverent contemplation of the common and everyday mysteries."
Here was disillusion without disenchantment; here was the paradox of a poet.

In this little book, too, he showed himself to be against violence in the solving of man's problems: he came out against
"bombs and brick-bats and broken skulls." (The poet's device
of alliteration was already useful.) He proposed instead "books
and pamphlets and speeches." Words might be "incidentals,"
but they were the civilized man's most justifiable weapons. Sandburg in 1904 was also a firm believer in the common mass of
men as the source of leadership—nothing hereditary, nothing
aristocratic. "The great man, the rare, strong, splendid individual who gives the world some great thought, some great action,
something of use, beauty, or inspiration, comes up from the mob,
springs from the vast mass of nameless, unknown individuals. . . .

The finer, healthier, brainier, and stronger you can make the mob, the mass of men, the greater the number of extraordinarily useful and sublime individuals you will produce." Almost a quarter of a century later he was to hold up Lincoln as the archetype of this kind of hero.

Sandburg said in *In Reckless Ecstasy* that his desire was to "be calm, unafraid and unwearied." He would want "to bring men hope and cheer and may be laughter pure as music." He prayed that he might be forever blessed with "the potencies of song and laughter." This idealistic strain he continued in *Incidentals*. He looked both at himself and at the human race: "I am an idealist. I can see humanity blundering on toward some splendid goal." And then a pronouncement foreshadows the scores of folk maxims in *The People, Yes:* "I don't know where I'm going but I'm on my way."

On the inside fold of the front cover he made a statement which he was to develop at greater length in 1928 in the definitions of poetry at the beginning of *Good Morning, America:* "We feel and see a thing before we study and explain it. Vision precedes analysis. That is why poets are as important as scientists." Observation and emotional reaction, then, would be his materials.

Several elements emerge in these two early pamphlets. First of all, a writer must recognize that words are his tools, that they are all he has to transmit his feelings, no matter how delicate and tenuous. Next, first-hand impressions are more valuable than ideas derived from reading. He was not inclined, either, to use the materials of others for his own purposes, except for the sayings of the plain people. Moreover, he was hoping to bring cheer where patently there was no cheer, and to maintain through all his own life an attitude at once tranquil, brave, and tireless. Finally, he was showing himself even at this early date (it would be a decade before he would have any public literary recognition) to have the cause of the common man at heart. He himself, as a common man, had the optimism of the adventurer on life; his goal was perhaps lost in the mists of the future, but his energy and determination were unmistakable. These were the themes he was intent on developing in his writing at this stage.

Writing was not his only interest. For some years he had been

playing a banjo to accompany his singing of songs of the laboring man and of the college student. Now he discarded it for a
guitar, which at first he tried tuned like a banjo but later learned
to play with normal tuning, though he never mastered more than
a few essential chords. Strumming accompaniment for himself,
he would sing the chanties and ballads he had gathered on his
travels. He had a deep, untrained voice, but one of profound
passion and of compelling virility. He began daily practices on
his guitar and learned to use his voice to good advantage as a
conscious artist.

When Wright published in 1906 a little book of his own, *The
Dreamer*, the professor asked his former pupil to write a foreword. Sandburg made use of the space to discuss the impossi-
bility of defining poetry, to consider the complexity of the poetic
act, and to promise an unlocked heart as the product of a genuine poem. "True poetry will . . . freshen and revivify your
every ambition and impulse for larger life." His idealism once
more manifested itself here: "Dream with the dreamer herein
his dreams. Some day we may weave them into realities." He
still signed himself "Charles A. Sandburg."

This teacher of his had undoubtedly been a force for good
in the young writer. In 1934, at Wright's death, Sandburg was
to testify: ". . . there never was a time when he did not deepen
whatever of reverence I had for the human mind. . . . He was
a great man and teacher in his profound influence on the potential young men with whom he came in contact." [7]

Cully Sandburg had known the small town and the prairie
countryside from babyhood. He had experienced life with
hoboes. He had seen poverty at close range, had known what it
meant to "make ends meet," and had cultivated sympathy for
the underprivileged. Hard work he had welcomed. Pride in
being himself, even at the expense of being misunderstood by
those who thought they knew him best, had become a thoroughgoing nonconformism. He had grown up in Lincoln territory and
had heard many a tale from men and women who had known
the Civil War President. He had cultivated a love of words, the
words of the common folk, both trite and imaginative. He had
become the close friend of a man of deep culture. He had seen
some of his own words in print. All these experiences were his
treasures, but they were not enough.

In 1906, in spite of his family and his professor friend, Sandburg at twenty-eight felt impelled to seek more stimulating adventures, social and intellectual, than Galesburg could offer. So he left town once more, and was never to return again except as a guest. He headed toward Chicago.

CHAPTER 2

The Lure of the Big City

I *Marriage and Socialism*

NOT LONG AFTER he had arrived in the Windy City, Sandburg was associate editor of *The Lyceumite,* a periodical of interest to platform artists who supplied lyceum and Chautauqua programs for communities large and small all over the nation. Sandburg wrote a series of thumbnail biographies of some of these performers, and, at an annual convention of the International Association, he even dared to give a talk about Whitman. It was a poor talk, and especially so for an audience of professional entertainers.

As early as 1904 he had thought of lecturing as a congenial way of making some money. He had advertised on one of the back pages of *Incidentals* the titles of three lectures he was prepared to deliver: "The Poet of Democracy: Walt Whitman" was a natural choice, for Whitman too had been a rover, a lover of people, a great patriot, and an expansive poet; "Civilization and the Mob" was a foretaste of his books to come; and "Bernard Shaw: Artist and Fool" was a harvest from his omnivorous reading. Only the Whitman lecture attracted any attention. Through the services of lyceum bureaus in Indianapolis and Pittsburgh, he was invited to deliver it several times in Indiana, Michigan, and Pennsylvania. But these early formal platform engagements were not extensive.

In the winter of 1907–8 he met in Chicago the state organizer in Wisconsin for the Social-Democratic party, Winfield R. Gaylord, who talked to him about the methods and goals of his party and offered him a job. Sandburg was moved by the party's idealism and by its firm stand for the betterment of the working classes. He had listened earlier with sympathetic ear to the tenets of the People's Party. Feeling as a boy that the conservatism of his father's Republicanism was unfair to the majority of the people, he had moved over into the Democratic camp. He now took another step: he accepted Gaylord's proposals, left *The Lyceumite* after almost a year, and moved to Milwaukee, where he received indoctrination in political techniques and became a district organizer for the Social-Democrats.

Though he was not on a formal payroll, he was lodged at the home of a local leader in the town where he was working and received about twenty-five dollars a month in collections made after his speeches. He wrote a few pamphlets propagandizing his party, the sale of which added possibly six or seven dollars to his monthly income; and now and then he would contribute an article to *La Follette's Weekly* which yielded him ten dollars. But that was all. Fortunately, his needs were modest. He never affected fine clothes, and simple food was good enough for him.

Very soon after he had gone to Wisconsin, he met Lillian Steichen—"Paula." From her home in Menominee Falls, where she was spending her Christmas vacation from her teaching position in the Princeton, Illinois, Township High School, she had come into Milwaukee one day to see Victor Berger, leading Socialist of the state and a member of Congress. They were consulting about Paula's translating some of Berger's German editorials into English. Sandburg happened to be in Berger's office at the time, offered to see Miss Steichen to her streetcar, and during that short walk fell in love. The young lady was a graduate of the University of Chicago, a member of Phi Beta Kappa, and an enthusiastic convert to Socialism.

The two young people began to exchange letters. When in early 1908 Paula wrote that she would be spending her spring holiday at home in Menominee Falls, Sandburg immediately invited himself to join her family for the occasion. He was not accepted by the family with enthusiasm: he did not have a really steady job, he wrote and read poetry (he carried Emerson, Whitman, and Shakespeare about with him), he was careless in dress; in other words, he was in general to be held somewhat suspect by a hard-working middle-class family. One exception was Paula's brother, Edward Steichen, who himself was not exactly following the pattern of his parents, for he was interested in photography as a career.

Paula returned to Princeton Township to finish out the school year, and Sandburg returned to his work for the Social-Democrats. As the word got around that he was given to writing poetry, sometimes he found the job of organization hard going. Men with calluses on their hands did not trust him, but he persisted; he was convinced of the validity of his party's principles. Throughout the remainder of the spring he traveled about the state and kept in constant touch with Paula. At the end of the school year, not quite six months after they had first met, they were married on June 15, 1908.

Paula gave up her teaching to devote herself to her husband. They moved to Appleton, where for four dollars a month they were able to rent a three-room, upstairs apartment. The house was owned by a Social-Democrat, of course—a workingman, a carpenter. Sandburg's income continued to be about the same, chiefly from passing the hat after his organization talks. Since Paula, however, was proving not only sympathetic but frugal, they got along. A beautiful woman of grace and simplicity, the new bride was blessed with seemingly endless energy. Her intellect had been well disciplined by university mathematics and the classics. She was indeed a godsend to the thirty-year-old idealist who had not yet actually found his place in the work of the world. Husband began to consult wife on every major decision— and has continued to do so ever since. He has said on various occasions that the three most important influences on his life have been Philip Green Wright, Edward Steichen, and the lovely Paula.

The young organizer's assignments in speech classes at college, his experience in the Erosophian Society, his lectures on Whitman—all were now contributing to greater ease before an audience. Reform was a condition of the times. Teddy Roosevelt was President. Lincoln Steffens, Upton Sinclair, Frank Norris, and Ida M. Tarbell were raking muck. Sandburg himself was caught up in the spirit. He became an evangelist of sorts, preaching the necessity for accident and unemployment insurance, for the assurance of a minimum wage, for the reduction of the working day to eight hours, for pension plans.

In 1909 he and Paula moved from Appleton to Milwaukee. Now in addition to his organizing activity with its precarious income, he began to write advertising for a department store. At night he practiced other writing—essays, sketches, editorials, poems. When he sent six tentative pieces to the Milwaukee *Journal*, in which his advertisements had appeared, he was given the opportunity to write features and an occasional news story. But he did not stay long with the *Journal*. With a seemingly ingrained restiveness, he went to the *Daily News* (as a substitute during vacation for one of the editorial writers), left it for the *Sentinel*, and at last returned to the *Journal*, for which paper he became a reporter at City Hall. Since the Social-Democrats had gained in strength and were nearing a majority on both the Milwaukee Common Council and the Board of Supervisors, Sandburg felt as if he were among friends in his new assignment.

While at City Hall he became acquainted with the Socialist leader Emil Seidel, who announced his candidacy for the office of mayor. Sandburg entered the campaign with the revivalist's passion that had become familiar to him, and he preached on street corners his gospel of a fair chance for the laboring man. The candidate was struck by his campaigner's enthusiasm for the cause, as well as by his intellectual understanding of the principles involved. When Seidel won the election and assumed the mayor's office in 1910, he appointed Sandburg his private secretary.

Here was still another world for the man from Galesburg to explore, the world of political favor. He discovered that his dreams of utopia, the ideal world he had pictured for his audiences at organization meetings, the leveled-out and equal civilization he had hoped for—all these were far removed from the actualities of life. He had to listen to complaints; he had to deal with the ambitious, both worthy and parasitic. Philosophy bore no relation to these problems of string-pulling, log-rolling, patronage, balance, and counterbalance. In *You and Your Job*, a pamphlet of his published in 1910 in Philadelphia by the Socialist Party, he observed: "The Socialist . . . knows the class-struggle is no bookish bubble-thing, but a reality of blood, sweat and tears, of desires and passions." (Had he and Winston Churchill both read Donne, or Byron, or Garibaldi?)

In 1910 Wright published at The Asgard Press in his basement still another booklet by Charles A. Sandburg, an appreciative essay about a poetic friend of his who chose to be known as "Joseffy." The theme of the pamphlet was the function of illusion. "We may go west for years only to find one day that we have been traveling east." Sandburg now felt that illusion was the base of "love and friendship and luck and poetry." As a matter of fact, he was learning in Milwaukee that life stripped of illusion can be pretty grim and grubby.

After about two years as secretary to Seidel, Sandburg became a labor reporter for yet another Milwaukee paper, the *Leader*. Since the Socialists were gaining in numbers almost daily, a liberal newspaper of the nature of the *Leader* had a good chance of survival. What Sandburg liked about his new job was that he was free to say what he wanted to. To please advertisers or a hard-nosed city editor was unnecessary.

II *Chicago and Poetry*

Again, however, he did not stay long with the *Leader*. A newspaper strike in Chicago had been like a bag of gold for one minority organ there, the *Daily Socialist*. Changing its name to the more noncommittal Chicago *World*, it increased its circulation to a phenomenal 600,000 and sent out a call for editorial and reportorial assistance. Several of the men from the Milwaukee *Leader* went down to help, including Sandburg, who moved Paula and their baby daughter, Margaret, into an apartment on Hermitage Street in Chicago.

Of course, as soon as the strike was over, the other papers regained business-as-usual status, and the circulation of the still-liberal *World* was drastically reduced. Out of work, in a new city and with a wife and child to consider, Sandburg at age thirty-four had to move fast. He found a job on the *Day Book*, a tabloid-size daily under the banner of E. W. Scripps. It carried no advertising and so was beholden to no man in its all-out support of the poverty-ridden worker. Sandburg was free to report exactly what he saw and to say exactly what his conscience dictated. The salary was set at twenty-five dollars a week.

But money can loom big in a man's life. Sandburg's next move proves the point: he went over to the enemy! The magazine *System* was designed for the edification of businessmen and industrialists. When that journal offered him an increase of ten dollars a week in salary, Sandburg became the associate editor. During the summer of 1913 he wrote three articles (for example, "Profit from 'Waste Space'"), in which he could not refrain from injecting occasional comments on the plight of the working man. To do so was to violate the policy of the magazine. Naturally he was asked to leave. But he landed on his feet—as editorial assistant in the offices of the *National Hardware Journal and American Artisan,* where he stayed for about six weeks.

Salary or no salary, the work was not to his taste. Towards the end of 1913 he was back at the *Day Book*—back at twenty-five dollars a week. There he could once more write stories pointing out the problems of strikers and exposing the causes of differences between labor and management. In other words, he could maintain his integrity.

He had been using more and more of his leisure to write poetry. Obviously under the influence of Whitman, he was composing for the most part in free verse. Sometimes he wrote as much as an entire poem in a day. Finally, about the first of the year 1914, he sent a sheaf of nine poems headed by "Chicago" to Harriet Monroe, whose monthly *Poetry: A Magazine of Verse,* though only a little over a year old, was developing a reputation for the brave support of little-known poets who wanted to be heard. Miss Monroe, who had "discovered" Vachel Lindsay, was looking for other promising unknowns.

When she read the opening lines of "Chicago," she was frankly shocked.[1]

> Hog Butcher for the World,
> Tool Maker, Stacker of Wheat,
> Player with Railroads and the Nation's Freight Handler;
> Stormy, husky, brawling,
> City of the Big Shoulders. . .   (*CP.* 3).

But she read on, and she soon sensed that a novel but authentic voice was sounding its barbaric yawp to her. This hoarse masculinity, however, was not all. The lines of "Jan Kubelik" were like the drawn-out phrases of a violin; "The Harbor" gently contrasted slums and lake; "Lost" created an unmistakable mood of loneliness. She decided to publish the group. They were on the first nine pages of the issue for March, 1914.

The effect was stormy. The loudest protest came from *The Dial*, which was now being published in Chicago and was trying to be literary arbiter for at least the Midwest. Said the reviewer: "The typographical arrangement for this jargon creates a suspicion that it is intended to be taken as some form of poetry, and the suspicion is confirmed by the fact that it stands in the forefront of the latest issue of a futile little periodical described as 'a magazine of verse.' . . . We think that such an effusion as the one now under consideration is nothing less than an impudent affront to the poetry-loving public." [2]

The writer's disdain might have dismayed a lesser person than Harriet Monroe, but she continued in her battle for freeing verse from nineteenth-century prettiness. She sent Carl Sandburg (he had by this time reverted to the Scandinavian name of his christening) a check for one hundred dollars; and, at the end of the year, she saw to it that he was awarded the Helen Haire Levinson Prize of two hundred dollars for the nine poems as the best of the year. (The money was used to pay the hospital bill for the birth of Carl and Paula's second daughter Janet.) For the first time in his thirty-six years he was realizing comparatively sizable sums from his poetry. He continued to write.

On March 1, 1914, because of the verses in *Poetry*, he was invited to a banquet for William Butler Yeats at the Cliff-Dwellers Club in Chicago, an event sponsored by Harriet Monroe with the backing of the guarantors of *Poetry* and some of the contributors. The guest of honor made some remarks that must have found sympathetic response in the heart of the newly recognized Midwest poet: "Poetry that is naturally simple, that might exist in the simplest prose, should have instantaneous effect, provided it finds the right audience. . . . The whole movement of poetry is toward pictures, sensuous images, away from rhetoric, from the abstract, toward humility. . . ." [3]

When Yeats had concluded, Vachel Lindsay chanted "The Congo" and, by request (Yeats had mentioned this poem particularly in his talk), "General William Booth Enters Heaven."

Edgar Lee Masters and Sandburg, two other Midwesterners who had met only a month or so before, also read from their poems. Sandburg contributed "Limited":

> Hurtling across the prairie into blue haze and dark air go fifteen all-steel coaches holding a thousand people.
>
> . . . .
>
> I ask a man in the smoker where he is going and he answers: "Omaha"   (*CP* 20).

Probably more self-conscious and certainly more cynical than Sandburg, the Irish guest wore an amused look according to Masters.[4] Sandburg had given his hearers the kind of simplicity one would find in unaffected prose. The irony of the smoking-car companion's reply may have escaped them.

With the impetus of prestigious—and paying—publication, Sandburg continued to compose verses. Sitting at his desk in the *Day Book* office, he wrote "Onion Days," a broad contrast between rich and poor. To while away the time in the waiting room of the judge of Juvenile Court, he wrote "Fog," an experiment more in the spirit than in the letter of the Japanese haiku; for his poem has six lines rather than three, twenty-seven syllables rather than seventeen. In May and again in November Miss Monroe published more poems by Sandburg. He was spending most of his evenings in the little apartment on Hermitage Street, which was now inadequate for the needs of his wife with a little girl and a baby to care for. Consequently, he moved his family to the suburbs, to Maywood (where they were to live for five years).

In the summer after his roaring appearance in *Poetry* he came into the County Building press room one rainy day with a friend of his, Jack Malloy, and asked if he could use the telephone to call the *Day Book* office. The "boys" continued their poker game until he had finished his call. Then Malloy said he would like them to listen to Sandburg read some of his verses. He rumbled through "Chicago," and then his tone changed:

> Three muskrats swim west on the Desplaines River.
>
> . . . .
>
> I lean on an ash and watch the lights fall, the red ember glow, and three muskrats swim west in a fan of ripples on a sheet of river gold.   (*CP*, 91)

His audience was city-toughened, but that evening it argued over the qualities of this new poet's work. Malloy placed it above Browning and Swinburne. Ben Hecht was thrilled by the way the commonplace was the center of focus. He was thoroughly moved, too, by the man's delivery—deep, passionate, but consciously controlled.[5]

Sandburg was in the right place at the right time. With the encouragement of Miss Monroe, a good many adventurers—including the "Imagists"—were breaking through the tyranny of the rules of metrics. In January, 1915, Ezra Pound himself wrote to the *Poetry* editor that he thought the new poet Sandburg had promise and a commendable purpose but that he did not yet know enough about writing.[6] Carl was gaining publication experience, was finding an audience that would read him, and was learning what his readers thought. No tyro could ask for more.

The following spring at a "Walt Whitman dinner" at the Grand Pacific Hotel, Ben Hecht, now one of Sandburg's loyal supporters, was bored by the lip service and basically unfelt tributes. Only Carl "sustained a dying faith in Walt, humanity, and *vers libre* in general." Carl stirred up considerable excitement with his Billy Sunday poem:[7]

> You come along . . . tearing your shirt . . . yelling about Jesus.
>> Where do you get that stuff?
>> What do you know about Jesus?
>
> .   —   .   .   .   .
>
> I like a man that's got nerve and can pull off a great original
>> performance, but you—you're only a bug-house peddler of
>> second-hand gospel—you're only shoving out a phoney imita-
>> tion of the goods this Jesus wanted free as air and sunlight.
>>> (*CP*, 29-30)

The poem was daring; the language was heady; the tone was a barrier-breaker; this righteous diatribe was throwing back at the notorious evangelist a little of his own sawdust.

These were stimulating days. In June, 1915, *Poetry* gave T. S. Eliot his first American audience with "The Love Song of J. Alfred Prufrock." In the autumn, Alice Corbin, Harriet Monroe's assistant, took a packet of Sandburg's poems to New York and left them with Alfred Harcourt, a salesman for Henry Holt and

Company, who had seen a few of the pieces a year before when he had been passing through Chicago. Sandburg himself was becoming acquainted with other writers: Vachel Lindsay, Sherwood Anderson, Theodore Dreiser. Margaret Anderson had launched her *Little Review,* which she edited with a high hand and which was, since it contained stories, plays, essays, and reviews in addition to a few poems, no competition for *Poetry.* In *The Little Review* were contributions from Sara Teasdale, Eunice Tietjens, Maxwell Bodenheim, Amy Lowell, Masters, Hecht, Anderson, Dreiser, Conrad Aiken—the list was a long one. These writers were all roused by a kind of Elizabethan explorer's curiosity about new lands to conquer. In April, 1916, Miss Anderson published four poems by Sandburg. He was in good company.

His new acquaintances did not necessarily subscribe to Sandburg's views wholeheartedly. Masters disagreed with his vision of Chicago: it was too narrow and unfair to the city itself.[8] Dreiser objected to his seeming passion for social change. Nor could he understand why Sandburg, so bold in other directions, shied away from the explicit in the exciting matter of sex, which was a fact to be faced in art in this newly frank post-Victorian time. Yet Dreiser had developed such an admiration for Sandburg that he tried to find a New York publisher for him. He felt that Sandburg had the rare secret of elegance amidst the commonplace, the ability to choose the precise word and put it in the right place, though the word might be vulgar in the eyes of the traditionalists.[9]

III *The First Book*

In the spring of 1916, about the time of Sandburg's first appearance in *The Little Review,* Holt published *Chicago Poems.* Alfred Harcourt had had to work very hard to convince the cautious editors that this was a worthy manuscript, one that did not lean on the past but was speaking to the future; at last he had won out.[10] When the volume appeared, Miss Monroe herself reviewed the collection in her magazine in May. There was heroism here, she said, whatever the mood. Like others who had listened to the man deliver his lines, she associated his manner and voice with what he had written: his *vers libre* was akin to his own "slow speech" and "massive gait." One could not deny the basic quality of honesty, "whether you call it poetry or not." [11]

And plenty of reviewers did not, especially as they read the slangy, colloquial lines of "To a Contemporary Bunkshooter," "Fellow Citizens," and "Mag." The quiet, descriptive verses were more to their taste. They were accustomed to the subject matter, the meters, and the rhymes they had inherited from the nineteenth century. True, Walt Whitman's *Leaves of Grass* had had some vogue; but Hecht had observed the year before how empty were the praises of that work. The verses of Father Tabb and Madison Cawein were more in line with what poets ought to be doing with words and rhythms. It had been twenty-two years since Edwin Arlington Robinson had made an almost anguished plea for a genuine poet who would rout the formalists and their routine sonnets,[12] but the right man had been slow in coming. At least one could not say that Sandburg was in the rut of tradition.

The Dial, naturally, took up its tirade of two years before. This man was "gross, simple-minded, sentimental, sensual," a "mystical mobocrat" first attacking, then lauding contemporary life. The little impressionistic poems were acceptable, however; in many instances they were even lovely. Another critic, William Stanley Braithwaite in the Boston *Transcript*, while conceding Sandburg's "tenderness" and "visual strength," branded *Chicago Poems* as "a book of ill-regulated speech that has neither verse nor prose rhythms." Though he was willing to admit that Sandburg had the imagination of a poet, Braithwaite denied in him any skill at communicating his vision to the reader.[13]

In fact all the reviewers—even those who thought his vision of the world was unfairly biased—acknowledged the great contrasts in Sandburg's tone. The predominantly brash "Chicago" was succeeded immediately by the delicate "Sketch" of a seascape. In the third poem, "Masses," he picked up the tone of pity which he had hinted at in "Chicago," where, however, it had been overridden by flexing of muscles and by pride in manhood. In the next poem, "Lost," he played on the theme of loneliness that was to come in again and again throughout his work. In "The Harbor" he contrasted the virtual imprisonment of the women in the slums with the energy and potential for freedom in nature.

In "They Will Say," though he admitted that this Chicago was *his* city, he had to repeat that it had its appalling, pitiful side. There was happiness, though, in spite of the limitations. Three poems in succession showed what happiness is: a fish crier gets as much pleasure from hawking his wares as does Pavlova from her dancing; an excursion boat returning after a day on Lake Michigan is gay with the music of a Polish brass band; a crowd of Hungarians spending Sunday along the Des Plaines River are happy drinking beer and listening to an accordion. And so the book went. Sandburg's people were primitives, their emotions uncomplex. When he was not expressing pride in the rough life of the poor, he was being protective of them in their suffering and deprivation.

The villains were the capitalists, who had taken more than their share of life's goods. This was why Sandburg hated Billy Sunday: he was in league with the oppressors. In "Onion Days" he told of an Episcopalian whiling away the time during a dull sermon in scheming how he could hire more girls to work for him at lower pay. Propaganda? Yes. After all, the poet had been an organizer for the Social-Democrats. He had given years to getting a fair chance for the laborer. His experience had made him a humanitarian to the point where he was inclined to distort by overemphasis the polarity of the suffering poor and the sinful wealthy and powerful. No poem in this book showed any sympathy with the problems of the middle and upper classes.

Despite the conservative critics, *Chicago Poems* was an adventure of considerable variety and novelty; related to the new poetic life of the Midwest, it was nonetheless produced by a distinctively individual voice. The verse itself departed widely from the customary: not only was there no rhyme, not even slant rhyme, but there was the greatest variation imaginable in line length—from a one-syllable word ("Now. . ." in "Clark Street Bridge" and "crawl" in "The Answer") to an entire poem written as a single paragraph-line of 139 words ("Bath"). Such structures were beyond conventional analysis. To establish a metrical pattern was out of the question. No wonder the reviewers were troubled.

Robinson had not understood why there was no real poetry in the 1890's, for the materials of poetry were still readily available. Sandburg here had certainly done away with the mechanisms of the sonnet, but he had also revitalized the subject matter of poetry: his people were men and women of the laboring classes; his flowers, seasons, and sunsets were those of the prairies and the Midwest cities for the most part. Even Robinson, whose *The Man Against the Sky* was published in this *annus mirabilis* of 1916, was still picturing the people of his native ground, the East, that had been exploited in American poetry for over two centuries. The Midwest was another matter. Only occasionally had this flat region been celebrated in verse, as in Bryant's "The Prairies" of over eighty years before. An almost unvarying broadness of landscape, a routine sort of history, cities devoted almost exclusively to industry, a people leading monotonous lives—these were the picture of the Central States in literary centers, thanks in part to the efforts of Hamlin Garland, Frank Norris, and Theodore Dreiser.

Whether consciously or not, Sandburg sensed that the spirit of Chicago could not be expressed totally in the confines of the usual lyric verse. The first poem, "Chicago," unlocked both language, form, and subject matter in a way that some critics found distasteful, some puzzling, and some invigorating. If he was virile in that poem, loud-mouthed in "To a Contemporary Bunkshooter," hard-pounding in the section of "War Poems (1914–1915)," elsewhere he was subtle, quiet, and abundantly musical (as in the section "Fogs and Fires").

In the opening poem Sandburg was saying this: Granted his city is evil (prostitutes work their trade), dishonest (killers are set free), and ruthless (women and children starve). Granted a tragic side to life, but another side gives compensation—vital and kinetic. Chicago is a masculine metropolis, affirming life by enterprising action, explosive curses, and laughter in the face of destiny. Slugging, fierce, and cunning in beating life at its schemes to get the best of the common man, Chicago has the instinct for taking enjoyment where it can be found.

The poet accepts both sides of this situation. The people may not have cultivated intellects and carefully nurtured manners, but they have a robustness and a blood-tingling pride that are necessary to the foundations of any healthy society. In return for this vitality, some people must suffer. (Is it not unfortunately necessary, on other levels, to have many fringe poets in order to produce a few great ones or to waste much in the economy to produce much?) Sandburg accepts the facts not only of suffering but also of the instinctive delight in being alive.

The "burden of destiny," however, he describes as "terrible," though man can do nothing about his plight but accept it and manage as he can with it. The mass, the people, are unthinking; but, in a sense, they experience a cosmic loneliness born of an unsolicited responsibility for making the most of a life thrust upon them. Their answer is to meet the smoke and dust of life, not with daintiness, modesty, and sedentary resignation, but with bragging, pulsating, ignorant, strong, unquestioning joy.

This poem has most of the qualities that Miss Monroe saw in the entire book: it has the essence of heroism; it is predominantly loud; but a suggestion of pity and delicacy appears: "On the faces of women and children, I have seen the marks of wanton hunger" (*CP.* 3). Insolence and braggadocio are grounded in compassion.

Despite comments from sneering critics, the poem is quite formal in structure. Essentially ternary, it makes a statement, takes off in departure, and ends in recapitulation. After the opening epithets comes a development section making use of parallelism, variety of line length, subtle shift of tone; then comes the recapitulation, the opening phrases in delicately shaded variation, now enriched by the central part of the poem.

At the ninth line, in the midst of the "departure" section, Sandburg makes a plain transition. Having admitted the evils of his city, he returns to the subject, the cause of the poem—the theme of rugged joy: "And having answered so I turn once more. . ." (*CP.* 3). This device of the mid-poem shift he uses in many pieces in the book. In "The Harbor" the first four lines describe the slum scene; then in the fifth line: "Out from the huddled and ugly walls/I came sudden. . ." (*CP.* 5). But here the structure is binary: there is no return to the opening statement. (It thus resembles the two parts of the center section of "Chicago.")

"Mamie" is another example of ternary structure. The girl is beating her head against the bars of a prison-like, small Indiana town, longing for "romance and big things." She escapes to Chicago, but she finds herself once more in a virtual prison, wondering if elsewhere she could find "romance and big things."

In "Cumulatives" Sandburg uses another source of coherence.

The Lure of the Big City

Here each of the three stanzas presents a subject for gossips to work on, decorate, add to. The order is climactic (that is, climactic from the point of view of the gossips): the subject of the first stanza is the comparatively impersonal one of ship-wrecks on a certain wind-beaten point of land; the second stanza concerns a has-been prize fighter and the admiration, or at least curiosity, he rouses; the final stanza—the juiciest item—is about a man whose third beautiful young wife resembles her two predecessors. The principle of arrangement is plain: increasing human interest from distant shipwreck to sports events to the complications of person-to-person relationships. Sandburg knows human nature; he knows that the dialogue of concern becomes more important to us as it draws closer to our daily lives.

"Cripple," another poem in binary structure, has thirteen lines divided at the sixth by a transition "I said to myself. . . ." The first five lines describe a tuberculosis victim slowly dying a tortured death in the slums. The last seven lines express the poet's preference for the life of a sunflower. Built on a favorite system of contrasts, the poem's two parts pair off words and phrases: "Cripple" and "tall sunflower," "gasping" and "living," "hollow eyes" and "golden-brown face." Whereas the cripple needs air, the sunflower is enjoying rain and dew; whereas the victim is "desperately gesturing," the sunflower is calmly watching the stars; "the dark and dust" of the tenement contrast with the majesty of the outdoors at night; the cripple's patent lone-liness is made more poignant by the sunflower's companionship with its own kind—poppies and hollyhocks. The theme emerges again in the contrast between the unwholesomeness of slum life and the freedom of a life in nature. In this poem the poet is saying he would rather not be a man at all than to have to suffer as this victim must. Far better to realize fulfillment as a sunflower (brief as a flower's life is) than to be born never to experience what man is potentially capable of—a rich emotional life in the freedom of the out-of-doors that is symbolized in the poem by "a country garden."

Many of the poems in the book are devoted not to contrast but to one circumstance, one mood, one picture. These were the days of the Imagists. Though Sandburg maintained stoutly that he was not of their school, he did say that he had been absorbing Japanese verse. Under its influence (in this respect like the

Imagists), he was unmistakably achieving the same effects of simplicity and clarity as H. D. or Amy Lowell.

The section headed "Fogs and Fires" contains "Nocturne in a Deserted Brickyard" and other gentle, imagistic etchings. These poems lack the underscoring, the shouting quality of the more startling compositions. They are inclined to look away from urban distinctions and to consider nature quietly but intensely. They are, on the surface, more like the roses-and-nightingales verse of the late nineteenth century than are the tougher ones.

Two of these pieces stand next to each other—"Monotone" and "Joy." The title of "Monotone" is ironically deceptive, for the immediate connotation could be somewhat unpleasant. But the three, three-line stanzas define beauty through three particularities; rain is beautiful, sunshine is beautiful, a certain woman's face is beautiful—as beautiful in its way (here the poem makes a return) as sunshine and rain. The fiery sun and the peaceful rain have proved to be symbols of passion and tranquillity in the woman's personality. Coherence is achieved through line-length (three- and four-beat), through similarity of first lines, and through the use of subject matter from the first two stanzas to develop the third.

> A face I know is beautiful—
> With fire and gold of sky and sea,
> And the peace of long warm rain.
> (*CP*, 51)

"Joy" is a single stanza of two- and three-beat lines (except the last, which is a four-beat line). More general than other "happiness" poems ("Fish Crier," "Picnic Boat," and "Happiness"), it generates rising excitement by the swift movement of its short line. The opening admonishment, "Let a joy keep you," becomes at the peak, "Let joy kill you!" The last line is a coda, a tapering off, a distillation of the wisdom of the poem: "Keep away from the little deaths." These are not only daily grievances but a final whimpering demise, both conquerable by a pervading spirit of joy (*CP*, 51).

"Fogs and Fires" and "Handfuls" are the sections that owe most to Emily Dickinson, whom Sandburg praises in a poem in still another section of earlier poems, "Other Days (1900–1910)." "Letters to Dead Imagists" is composed of two three-line tributes, one to Emily ("You gave us the bumblebee who has a soul") and the other to "Stevie Crane" (". . . we never knew the kindness of war till you came" [*CP*, 73]).

Sandburg's own "War Poems (1914–1915)" are geared to the ruthlessness, the suffering, and the ultimate uselessness of war. One recalls his early advocacy of words instead of bombs for the settling of international disputes. These poems, however, are percussive in effect; they follow the merciless, pounding pattern of battle. "And They Obey"—not a subtle poem, but one showing a feeling for structure (the two five-line stanzas are parallel)—develops the two themes of war's futility and of the people's patient endurance:

> Smash down the cities,
> Knock the walls to pieces. . . .
>
> Build up the cities.
> Set up the walls again. . . .
> (*CP*, 40)

The idea of the great masses moving on through time like a mighty and irresistible river was to take over more and more of Sandburg's thinking in his poetry until, in 1936, he was to produce almost a sociological treatise. The most explicit preliminary statement in this book occurs in "Other Days." Called "I Am the People, the Mob," it defines the mass as laborer and as witness to history. The implied criticism is that the mass is inclined to forget its grievances. In that far-off day when the mob can manage to remember the evils it has borne, it will take command of the world. Of course, this social idealism informs almost every page of the book. One knows where the poet's sympathies lie.

Other themes come to the surface in *Chicago Poems*. Two are of particular interest here. The first is concerned with the limitations of the written word; the second, with the inevitability of change, of death, and of ultimate silence.

In "Onion Days" Sandburg comments on the ultimate inadequacy of drama or fiction to convey profound emotions. After taking a look at the demoralizing future of some poor, proud, innocent Italian woman whose destiny is in the hands of an exploiting Episcopalian millionaire, the poet says his acquaintances think the people of this situation would be good characters in a novel or a play. Sandburg himself expresses no confidence in the ability of any playwright to convey accurately the assurance and simple, present happiness of Mrs. Gabrielle Giovannitti (*CP*, 14).

This is a shallow view. If he were thinking, as he wrote these last lines, of the American theater of his time (that is, before Eugene O'Neill), he was right. Depths of happiness with over-tones of threatening destruction, however, occur in many places in literature, and successfully. Sandburg himself surely did not despair of his own efforts in this very book—in "Dynamiter," "Ice Handler," and "Jack," to name only three instances in which, through concrete image, he had given his reader effective sym-bols of the subjects' emotion. An example is "He died in the poorhouse sitting on a bench in the sun. . ." (*CP*, 22). Even at the moment of death, this pauper had been tranquil and full of optimism. Possibly Sandburg had the humility about the inadequacy of art when confronted with the primitive that Yeats mentioned, but such a defeatist view was not typical of the Sandburg assurance.

After his first appearance in *Poetry* Sandburg had been made aware that his somewhat crude break with convention was hard for many serious readers of poetry to take. He answered these critics in "Style," the burden of which is that style is an indi-vidual matter, whether it be that of a dancer, a baseball player, or a writer. An artist will do what he must. Even if it is bad, it is his own; and he must bet on it. It is his "face," that with which he confronts the world. To imitate others is to die as an artist.

> Kill my style
> > and you break Pavlowa's legs,
> > and you blind Ty Cobb's batting eye.
> > > (*CP*, 24)

In "Bath" (which, like "Onion Days," one is hard put to classify as a poem) Sandburg demonstrates the power of rebirth in the experience of art. A disillusioned and cynical man views life as a trap until he hears a glorious concert by Mischa Elman, after which he is transformed. He appears the same, he lives the same life, but his view is affirmative; he has been cleansed of his mocking vision. Now not only does he accept life's vicissitudes, but he loves them. To its sensitive witness and participant, art has the power of renascence (*CP*, 26).

Ars longa est. In "Bronzes" Sandburg senses a disregard for the statue of General Grant during the hustle of daytime money-getting, but at night, when a storm is on the lake, it assumes a daring strength, as if willing to do battle with the storm. Against the winter snows the statues of Lincoln (in Chicago's Lincoln Park), of an Indian, of Shakespeare, and of Garibaldi will hold their own and outlast the night (*CP*, 27).

In spite of a primary feeling of inadequacy in art, then, poetry is Sandburg's medium of expression, that with which he must *try* to interpret life. Furthermore, he must be permitted to do it in his own way, to let his style grow out of his personality, experience, and subject matter. Then, too, all around him is plenty of evidence that art has a useful function—a function of refreshment and even of rebirth of the spirit. And finally, art endures—a testimony to the quality of a civilization.

One sees the beginning of Sandburg's dilemma: he was speaking for the masses, he would have liked to be one of them, yet he could not be; for as artist he had to maintain his individuality and to refine and cultivate his senses in a way totally alien to the people as a whole. From the beginning, however, he had committed himself to the myth of the ultimate efficacy of the people; and in this book he had been distorting the position of the well-to-do—as much through omissions as through positive statements—in order to emphasize his own sympathies with the laboring classes. This was nothing short of propaganda for a socialist utopia, as Dreiser had seen. As art (one must be candid), it often fails because it descends into plodding prose reiterations of the obvious or into sentimentality—as when he writes in "Masses" of the sociological mass as being "more patient than crags, tides, and stars."

He had written a poem defending the right of an artist to cultivate and bank on the style that seems to him to be organic to his material. For Sandburg the freedom of line length was appealing, a release from the restriction of set traditional stanza patterns. For him, too, language should know no bounds. What was suitable for one subject and mood would be totally inappropriate elsewhere.

Paula is digging and shaping the loam of a salvia,
   Scarlet Chinese talker of summer.
Two petals of crabapple blossom fallen in Paula's hair,
   And fluff of white from a cottonwood.

                  (*CP*, 55)

This poem, "June," is more than a flat drawing of his wife. Its
language makes it tranquil and pleasantly industrious without
compulsion.

> You slimy bunkshooter, you put a smut on every human blossom
> in reach of your rotten breath belching about hell-fire and
> hiccupping about this Man who lived a clean life in Galilee.

                  (*CP*, 30)

This outburst answers vulgarity with vulgarity. "Mag," on the
other hand, is in the language of a working man caught in the
despair of poverty and a large family:

> I wish to God I never saw you, Mag.
> I wish to God the kids had never come.

                  (*CP*, 13)

Sandburg made conscientious effort to achieve the very thing
he had said in "Onion Days" could not be done—to capture
through language, arrangement, and rhythm the mood and
theme of his material. In many instances he was highly successful in this first book.

Another recurring theme cluster relates evanescence, death,
and silence. The people as a force might move on through the
centuries, but as individuals they must undergo the same fate
as their generals and demagogues. This theme of passing time
hovers over the entire book, from the "burden of destiny" of the
mass in "Chicago" to "Nobody knows where she's gone" in
"Gone" (a poem about a "fast" girl, Chick Lorimer [*CP*, 64]).
The small imagistic poems in the section marked "Handfuls"
are a case in point. In "Crimson" the glow and ash of a cigar
suggest the death of a great man. In "Losses" a sweetheart, a
child, a sweet strumming banjo—all must go. There will be only
shadows left.

Among the "War Poems" a soldier in "Murmurings in a Field
Hospital" longs for what is past. He recalls a singing woman in

a garden of hollyhocks, poppies, and sunflowers (this cluster of flowers occurs also in "Cripple"), and an old man telling fantastic stories to children. To his mind comes the image of a crock of new butter in a window framed with roses. The pathos lies in his present shrapnel-ridden condition in contrast with scenes from childhood: "And the world was all playthings" (*CP*, 38).

For the individual at last the answer is death—and silence. In "Black-listed" the central figure is suffering from alienation. He has the freedom to take another name in order to get a job for survival—freedom because no one cares, either his fellows or God Himself. The man is dead, is no longer what he was. More directly, in "The Right to Grief" Sandburg finds Death a fact anywhere; no amount of money can buy him off. In this poem the writer shows a slight petulance: others may choose to elegize the death of a rich man's child, but "if I want to," I can cry over someone else. The poor child's family mourns not so much at the loss of the child—though it has had concern throughout her sickness—as at the idea of the imminence of death for them all. They sob when they hear the formula: "God have mercy on us all"—a sentimental, stock response, but an articulation of man's plight, of which they are only half aware. In the conclusion of this poem Sandburg gets in a bit of propaganda: in proportion, the rich child's funeral costs its father nothing; it will take the stockyards menial, however, at least six months to pay the undertaker's fees in weekly installments. But when the funeral is over, all is silence: the monotony of everyday living begins again, and in its way it is a relief—a screen hiding the ultimate problems of suffering and death (*CP*, 12–13).

In "The Answer" no answer comes—only silence. The pushing up, burgeoning, and blooming of a pansy makes the poet realize that it did not come from a first-suspected "nowhere," but from a really more awful "silence," which Sandburg equates also with the future, that is, the answer—indefinable but inevitable. The poem begins with human beings, "you" and a "child," then moves into the universe; and finally it returns to the observable pansy, which is just as miraculous as the cosmos. Everything comes out of that silence—the future, the unknowable—which, however, is always at work producing the present (*CP*, 45–46).

The last poem in the book, written before Sandburg had come

to Chicago to stay, is called "Gypsy." The woman's word of
wisdom, old as an obelisk on the Nile, is "silence":

> Snatch off the gag from thy mouth, child,
> And be free to keep silence.
> Tell no man anything for no man listens,
> Yet hold thy lips ready to speak.
>
> (*CP*, 76)

He had used the obverse idea a few years earlier when in
Incidentals he had said: "Were I a sculptor carving a figure to
symbolize the power of print and speech, it would be a stately
goddess with her lips parted in plea and utterance. On the
pedestal, I would inscribe, 'I will be the Word of the People.
Mine is the bleeding mouth from which the gag is snatched.
I will say everything!' Everything is possible, yes. But to man
not all things are possible." Man has his limitations; he does not
know the answers; but he can and must search.

The poet can observe and record; he can try to recreate
experience and feeling; but in the long run he cannot give a
reply; he can only ask the questions. He does not know the
answers any more than any one else, and if he did, no one
would listen. But he is obligated to be ready. For one day the
answers may come to him, and in a golden utopia mankind may
be prepared to hear what he has to say.

Nearly a hundred and fifty poems crowded the pages of this
first book. They had broken the stultifying patterns of conservative poets and of timid poetasters. They had dared to open up
"unpoetic" areas of life as material for poetry. Some of them
were sentimental; some prosy, dull, and shapeless; but the best
were strong with an appropriate harshness or gentle with a
suitable limpidity. A new voice of promise had arisen, a possible
fulfillment of Whitman's call for a truly democratic poet, an
iconoclast no longer bound by the empty sonnet form Robinson
had decried.

CHAPTER 3

A Growing Reputation

I *Europe*

DESPITE SOME NEGATIVE REACTIONS, enough good and understanding things had been said about *Chicago Poems* to give the poet encouragement. He continued to write and to publish. He liked to drop in at the *Poetry* office for a talk with Harriet Monroe, Alice Corbin, and any other contributors who might also be there. He was becoming well known among the Chicago makers of literature. And he had made an impression on the workers he wanted to represent, for the organizers of the American Federation of Labor often carried copies of his book in their kits and read a selection or two at their meetings. This kind of poetry was not suspect; it was trimmed of all decoration that the people found useless; it had a purpose, their purpose.

In 1917 Scripps closed down the *Day Book*. During wartime, he felt energies should be directed toward the winning of the cause. The less internal strife the better. The policies of the liberal *Day Book* were for the time irrelevant, its purposes too experimental.

Sandburg's weekly salary had been raised to $27.50 a week. He had been faithful in reporting what he saw—for example, a fifteen-week strike of the Amalgamated Clothing Workers and other disputes involving the problems of labor. He tried to give the common man a fair say. Furthermore, he found other outlets for his talents as contributing editor of the *International Socialist Review*. When in his zeal he found himself author of several articles in a single issue, he used other names besides his own. With a wife and two little daughters to provide for, he ate lightly and cheaply at noon and in the evening walked the two miles from the end of the trolley line to his home.

In July, after the *Day Book* had ceased publication, he hired himself out to the liberal National Labor Defense League as a trouble-shooter. He went to St. Louis and to Omaha to help untangle the knotty threads of exploitation in the hands of profiteers.

> Here in Omaha
> The gloaming is bitter
> As in Chicago
> Or Kenosha.
>   (*CP*, 89)

In three weeks he was back in Chicago, briefly with the Hearst *Evening American* and then at the more congenial *Daily News*.

The loyal Ben Hecht was on the *Daily News* staff and had recommended Sandburg to the managing editor, Henry Justin Smith, with the warning that he was a man of genius not to be pushed too hard. Smith was sympathetic and took the chance. For the most part, Sandburg's stories turned out to be unorthodox; they were sometimes late; sometimes they did not get in at all. But Smith cautioned the city editor to be patient, as he was—outwardly.[1]

On October 2, 1917, Sandburg published an interview he had had in jail with Big Bill Haywood, the Chicago leader of the Industrial Workers of the World. A week later, however, he made it clear in a story that he was not at all in accord with the efforts of the Socialists to sabotage the war effort, either by strike or by violence. Like Scripps, he was of the firm opinion that, once America was committed to conflict, her citizens were bound to strive for victory. He and Paula left the Socialist party which they had staunchly supported for a decade. They saw no way out but for America to join the Allies. Sandburg was now politically an independent, but through the years he was more frequently to support the Democratic party than the Republican.

Late in the summer of 1918 the *Daily News* sent him to the East to cover a labor union convention. When in New York he caught sight of American soldiers leaving for the European battle front, he had a desire to become a war correspondent. Approached by the Newspaper Enterprise Association to report the revolution in Finland, he applied for a passport, agreed to seventy-five dollars a week and expenses, and felt that he would now be near the vital conflict. Before his ship left, he walked the streets of New York soaking up sights and sounds—Broadway, Fifth Avenue, the Lower East Side. Then he was off to Christiania and Stockholm. He was gone for nearly five months.

II *Cornhuskers*

While he was still abroad, at the very end of 1918, Holt published his second book of verse, *Cornhuskers*. Its reception was not so stormy as its predecessor's had been. Two more years of *vers libre* had attuned more ears to its irregularities. And the general tone of this book was not so brash, insolent, and shocking. The poet was now turning his attention away from the noise of the metropolis toward the comparative tranquillity of the rolling prairie he had known as a boy, but he still let notes of protest be heard.

The fact that Sandburg was forty years old, already at midlife, was significant; for *Cornhuskers*, on the whole, was somewhat less unthinkingly optimistic than *Chicago Poems*. An autumnal nostalgia haunted almost every page, due in part to his vague Scandinavian heritage of mysticism and in part to the fact that he was no longer a young man. The buoyancy was still present, but it was tempered by an obviously increasing awareness of the passing of time and by other sobering thoughts.

Sandburg had turned his major attention away from urban Chicago toward the broad Midwest countryside in which he had grown to manhood. A few "city" poems occurred, but their subjects were not so often Chicago as other large places he had come to know in his travels—Omaha or Buffalo. He was still an American poet, and his pieces were about America and her people; but he was outgrowing any tendency to provincialism. The brutality of "Chicago" was missing, but cast-iron knucks were offered for sale in Springfield, the city of the man who had advocated "malice toward none." The strong pity of "The Harbor," the loud anger of "To a Contemporary Bunkshooter," the loaded irony of "Onion Days"—all were modified.

In writing of Joliet, Sandburg emphasized the valley setting of the little city. In "Slants at Buffalo, New York" he focused on art and color: a sculptured shaft, the bright reds, greens, and yellows in a delicatessen, the blue of the lake, the white of the sun. He recalled from his Omaha visit the coming of evening, which he described with a characteristic combination of elevated language and slang: "The long sand changes,/Today is a goner" (*CP*, 89).

A few etchings of the working classes remind the reader of the writer's basic sympathies, but the pictures rise neither from sorrow nor from indignation. The "Girl in a Cage" sometimes enjoys fingering the money she dispenses. She wears "A flame of rose in the hair,/A flame of silk at the throat" (*CP*, 106). Sandburg was not obsessed any longer by the six-dollar-a-week salesgirls. And Greek ditch diggers in "Near Keokuk" work very hard, naturally, but they take their pleasure in their noon lunch breaks. The poet puts them in an almost idyllic situation: they "are dipping their feet in a creek,/Sloshing their bare feet in a cool flow of cold water" (*CP*, 117). In *Chicago Poems* he had shown the poor in their modest joys, enjoying temporary surcease from their labors. Two years later he was still trying to achieve a definition of primitive "happiness."

In another direction, the slamming frustration of the earlier "Mag" becomes in "Bricklayer Love" a despairing resignation. The three lines of this poem are very long; they have lost the telegraphic tone. The language is no longer staccato. Though most of the words are monosyllabic, the consonants are not so explosive as in "Mag" (*CP*, 127).

Sandburg had softened, then, both the materials and the language of protest and pity. A larger cosmic relationship begins to show itself, as in "Leather Leggings":

> They have taken the ball of earth
> and made it a little thing.
>
> . . . . . .
>
> Under the sea
> and out to the stars
> we go.
> (*CP*, 108-9)

In "Always the Mob" he sounded his familiar note of the people as the great continuing stream out of which rise the leaders, as well as the ordinary mortals; but his ideology was not so fierce. Indeed, it was tempered by a vision of man's relation to the universe, by what he now saw as inevitable mysteries and sorrows:

> One more arch of stars,
> In the night of our mist,
> In the night of our tears.
>   (*CP*, 111)

The hardest pounding of language in *Chicago Poems* had been in "Chicago," in "To a Contemporary Bunkshooter," and in a few war poems. In this second book, any insistent percussive quality occurs in three poems of quite differing tone. "Prayers of Steel" puts hard verbs ("beat," "hammer," "pry," "drive") to use by re-creating the intensity of vigorous activity in tearing down the old and constructing the new. In these lines is the "Chicago" impatience with the outmoded, a red-hot desire to build—the American motif. Taken altogether the poem may also be broadened into an urgent prayer for fulfillment—for effective creation of personal essence, realization of potential. It too ends on a note of cosmic recognition: "Let me be the great nail holding a skyscraper through the nights into white stars" (*CP*, 110). This relation of man and his works to the heavens—and what it might thus signify—crops up on many pages of this book.

"The Four Brothers" is a second poem making extensive use of explosive diction. It is a war poem, or rather "Notes for War Songs (November, 1917)" (*CP*, 143–47). France, Russia, Britain, and America are the brothers. Again indicating a shift of emphasis in Sandburg, the mood is not so much one of protest as of necessity and determination. Once committed, the brothers must carry on. The words are made to serve that imperative mood.

> Cowpunchers, cornhuskers, shopmen, ready in khaki;
> Ballplayers, lumberjacks, ironworkers, ready in khaki;
> .   .   .   .
> They are hunting death,
> Death for the one-armed mastoid kaiser.

Following a technique he had established in the first book (and even in the verses in *Poetry* before the book itself), Sandburg again was mingling patois and convention, slang and elegance: he wrote: "Of a half-cracked one-armed child of the German kings." Then he concluded in lyric optimism with a vision of the future when all wars shall cease and the world's people will be secure: "Under the chimneys of the winter-time the children of the world shall sing new songs."

The third poem, "Gargoyle," uses hard verbs and nouns too: "jeering," "rattling," "fist," "hit," and "pounding." The effect is violent, almost as violent as anything in *Chicago Poems;* but the exact significance is elusive. Since the poem is included in a section made up principally of pieces on the theme of war, it may be related to them. Whatever its immediate subject matter, it assuredly is a poem of destruction, whether for good purpose remains ambiguous: "The fist is pounding and pounding, and the mouth is answering" (*CP*, 137).

Some of the reviewers of *Cornhuskers* remarked on the generally less professionally male diction, though the *Review of Reviews*, having groped for a parallel between *Chicago Poems* and "a statue of Rodin," persisted in affirming "the vitality and strength of the English tongue as it was in its beginnings." O. W. Firkins, always disdainful of Sandburg's work, called his language and mood, in contrast with the first book, "the difference between black smoke and blue"; he added that Sandburg was as yet insufficiently oriented toward the blue smoke of the idyllic. More in sympathy with what Sandburg was trying to do, Louis Untermeyer admired the poet's way of mingling "cheapness and nobility," of using "proper names and slang" creatively. These professional readers did not feel any slackening of energy; they simply felt that the vocabulary was more controlled, not so strained, in the effort to achieve manly effect. The poet did not have to be merely cacophonous to communicate intensity.[2]

Part of the reason for the subduing of the brashness and harshness found in the poems of the first volume is that the scene for the most part has changed from the hustle, the screeching poverty, and the oppression of the metropolis to the less hurried pace and greater general prosperity of the smaller cities and the open fields. These were Sandburg's native ground; these were the symbols of his faith, the Populist-Socialist-Democratic credo of a fair chance for all. Word choice follows subject matter appropriately. Actually, Sandburg had not changed the character of the diction: for example, the imagistic nature etchings of *Chicago Poems* were achieved with precisely the same kind of language as he used in this book in "Young Bull-frogs," "Sixteen Months," and "In Tall Grass." There were simply fewer poems requiring violent diction than in the earlier book. This is why the tone of the collection was quieter.

In the structure of his pieces the poet of *Cornhuskers* continued to ignore the restrictions of traditional verse forms. As for variety of line length, only two poems contain a one-word line—"Southern Pacific" and "The Four Brothers." This reduction is related to the less explosive, less telegraphic, less angry mood of the entire book. Even in "Southern Pacific" the three syllables of "Huntington" do not burst out, though the single word itself creates a thoughtfully ironic effect in juxtaposition with "Blithery," one of the railroad laborers:

> Huntington,
> Blithery, sleep in houses six feet long.
> (*CP*, 105)

On the other hand, the two-word line is common, again for emphasis, as in "Humdrum":

> —would you?
> or you?
> or you?
> (*CP*, 120)

Not only repetition and brevity but arrangement contribute to the effect. And again Sandburg used the single long paragraph (as in the earlier "Bath") for the structure of "Summer Shirt Sale"; and whether this is a poem is not the point. Except for the much less frequent use of the one-word line, no change or refinement in line-length or stanzaic form from *Chicago Poems* is discernible.

In the organization of materials, the poet in *Cornhuskers* gave up virtually altogether the device of mid-poem transition (which he had used, for example, in "The Harbor"). More and more he made use of the rhetorical device of repetition. In the first stanza of "Southern Pacific" all three lines begin with "Huntington"; in the second, with "Blithery." All six lines of "Questionnaire" begin with "Have I." All five lines of "Kreisler" begin with "Sell me." And within many other poems, whole series of lines begin with identical words. The effect is that of a chant (one of Sandburg's own categories of poetry).³ If criticism finds this device an easy way out for the problem of securing coherence, the fact remains that Sandburg had a much-admired precursor in Whitman, whom he had studied carefully. A variation of the repetition technique occurs with leveling irony in "Cool Tombs," where each of the four stanzas *closes* with a two-phrase refrain, quietly intense:

> Pocahontas' body, lovely as a poplar, sweet as a red haw in November or a pawpaw in May, did she wonder? does she remember? . . . in the dust, in the cool tombs?

> Take any streetful of people buying clothes and groceries, cheering a hero or throwing confetti and blowing tin horns . . . tell me if the lovers are losers . . . tell me if any get more than the lovers . . . in the dust . . . in the cool tombs (*CP*, 134).

The two major poems (if length can be the criterion) employ most of Sandburg's favorite mechanisms. "The Four Brothers" is the lone example of a structure clearly divided by a transitional phrase "Well . . ." The first part of the poem describes France, Russia, Britain, and America as fighting because fighting is the only way out—to defeat the Kaiser. After the "Well . . ." comes a hopeful conclusion, an assuring assertion that God is not the God of despots: "God is a God of the People."

The limitations of Sandburg's vision are evident in this poem, and echoes of his early interest in Populism reverberate. The poet had the narrow view of a professional patriot in wartime. The armies of the Allies represent the "People." No notion is present that God might also be the God of the German people. The idea that the true enemy is Kaiser Wilhelm may be sound enough, but the unconsidered concept is that the Allied armies are fighting the common people of the other side, who also swear *Gott mit uns*. Incomplete as his view was in this poem— too simple, too unqualifiedly patriotic, in a word, too journalistic—Sandburg was vivid in his conclusion; with a few strokes he drew a ghastly enough picture of a war that will bring at last a lovely, singing peace: "The four brothers shall be five and more."

The other long poem, "Prairie" (*CP*, 79–85), introduces the book and sets the characteristic tone, just as "Chicago" did for *Chicago Poems*. Though it is among the longest pieces the poet ever wrote, it does not ramble; it holds together through a symmetry that shows consciousness of the problem of structure on Sandburg's part without yielding to mathematical and mechanical exactitude. The five divisions are marked by shifts in point of view: the first six lines belong to the poet as a son of the prairie; the next ten lines are ambiguous, could belong to Sandburg, to the prairie, or to neither; the great middle section (ninety-three lines) is the prairie speaking; the fourth part (nineteen lines) is again ambiguous as to *persona;* and finally, nine lines again in Sandburg's own voice bring the poem to a close. Mechanically, the poet used ellipsis periods to divide parts of the poem from each other, there being several sections within the five main divisions.

Not only in symmetry of lengths and *persona* does the conscious artist show himself at work, but in coherence of subject matter also. A definite progression of thought helps build tension. At the beginning Sandburg expresses his feeling of belonging to the prairie. He possesses a sense of its geological history, of its present geographical boundaries (east and west), and of its sky above (north and south). He states his own desire for another dawn or evening, simply "tomorrow" without great dependence on history or particular plans for the future. This is a point he comes to again with various refinements—that the present is what counts.

In the second section seven lines—vigorous, quick-moving— detail a farm worker's day and pleasant evening; and two long lines (a train moving through the countryside) contrast the cramped, evil milieu of the city with the wide-open freedom of the prairie. Sandburg's molding of the length of line to amplify his meaning is the work of an artist. (He had used the long, sinuous line in "Jan Kubelik" to give the feeling of the drawn-out melody of a violin.)

Variety of line length is useful, too, in the third or long center section that is devoted to the prairie itself. Subject matter and tone avoid monotony without betraying the pervading mood. The five introductory lines begin with "I" to establish the *persona* of the prairie. They outline the poet's principal ideas about it: it precedes and survives civilizations; it supports both pioneers and the current citizenry; and it becomes the burial place of all such men. The rest of the section plays variations on these themes: Indians, pioneers, wars—all pass; farming, prairie, cities, industry, railroads, uncomplicated private life—all make the present fascinating; but in the long run all these things are evanescent, and the prairie waits to engross them wholly. This section ends with a passage on corn husking—an activity of autumn, the time of memories: ". . . falltime, leaves, bonfires, stubble, the old things go and the earth is grizzled."

The fourth section moves from the phantom recollections inspired by fall to prairie music—

> mocking birds
> Flinging follies of O-be-joyful
> Over the marshes and uplands

and to women in the kitchen—but it ends on a note of sympathy for the lonely prairie girl whose lover has gone away.

As he himself returns in the final section, Sandburg testifies once more to his love of the prairie, and he concludes the poem with avowal of faith in the present and in a vague tomorrow. He makes it clear at this point that he puts no stock in the value of history: "I tell you the past is a bucket of ashes." He states no tenets of a definable creed, but holds to the amorphous belief that progress is the answer, a mist-shrouded optimism. At least he supports a looking ahead, which is more wholesome than a morbid obsession with the past. Nostalgia of a sort, however, a preference for the fading glories of October, pervades the entire poem.

Thoreau concludes *Walden* on an up-beat: "Only that day dawns to which we are awake. There is more day to dawn. The sun is but a morning star." A difference between Thoreau and Sandburg is that the Concord man advocated a definite program of adventuring on life and had his thinking profoundly established in history. It would never have occurred to Thoreau to consider the past as merely "a wind gone down." Sandburg intended his poem to end on a bravely pioneering note, but the reader must ask where the poem leaves man. If what is behind him is empty and what is ahead is only a child's anticipation of another day, where is man? Teetering on the point of a pin, unfed by history or philosophy? Because of this failure to come to grips with man's fate, either fore or aft, Sandburg was skimming the surface, did not achieve profundity, was always asking the questions without really searching for the answers.

Though in poetry a reader looks for much more than a stated idea, he hopes for flashes of insight built soundly on a fairly articulate world view. Rarely did Sandburg come even close to this achievement. Hence he was at his best in the short poem or passage. He could not sustain an idea and give it dynamic depth through a piece of any length. In the present case, "Prairie" has a coherent structure, true enough, but the poem is only of medium length, and its interest lies in the symmetry of its architecture and its impressions of "mother" prairie. What Sandburg might have developed he sacrificed by his shrug of the shoulders at the end. Despite her geological age and the misty hopes for a tomorrow, it is what the prairie is today, and today only, that Sandburg accepted in the last analysis.

It is only fair to say, however, that the Sandburg poem comes out well by comparison with William Cullen Bryant's frequently anthologized account of his first sight of the Midwest. "The Prairies," written in 1832, when the poet was thirty-eight, bears some superficial resemblance to Sandburg's work. It is shorter by only a dozen lines than "Prairie." It is the work of a man approaching middle age. It, too, touches upon the past, present, and future. And there is no rhyme.

The first difference is that the blank verse of Bryant gives his poem a traditionally foregone dignity, suitable to the nobility and the vastness of the scene, to the poet's funereal interest in its past, and finally to a brief picturing of a well-ordered, conventional future. Deeply affected by a sight the like of which he had never before experienced, Bryant was nevertheless an outsider. The tone to which the unrhymed pentameters contribute is steadily dispassionate; it is beyond the impulsive excitement of a younger man. (Of course, "Thanatopsis" has much the same quality—an exception to the usual juvenilia.)

Sandburg's poem has much more variety. It changes pace frequently and grows out of a different attitude from Bryant's— the attitude of a man of prairie origin. Written when Sandburg was forty, it no longer shows the brawny quality of "Chicago," the desperate petulance of "Mag." Again, subject matter may have something to do with tone, but even such lines as

And the men in the rolling mills with their shirts off
Playing their flesh arms against the twisting wrists of steel . . .

are tempered by the short speculative lines which follow:

what brothers these
in the dark
of a thousand years?

Bryant looks into the future:

from the ground
Comes up the laugh of children, the soft voice
Of maidens, and the sweet and solemn hymn
Of Sabbath worshippers; low of herds
Blends with the rustling of the heavy grain
Over the dark-brown furrows.

Sandburg's picture of fulfillment, on the other hand, is not so totally rural and peaceful as Bryant's prophecy. His particularities give his total poem a greater realism than the skimming generalities and the easy clichés that Bryant had inherited from such English predecessors as Gray, Goldsmith, and Wordsworth. Sandburg is successful in adapting vocabulary, rhythm, and line length to meaning with a more dramatic result than was possible in the staid iambic pentameters of Bryant. The basic idea of "Prairie" may not be profoundly articulated or even significant, but the communication of variety of emotion is eminently successful.

The ternary device of recapitulation of opening phrases at the end as a means of enclosing the poem (as in "Chicago") is not so frequent in *Cornhuskers*. "Upstairs" and "Smoke" use exact repetition. "Interior" closes with a rearrangement and echo of opening phrases. But other patterns of organization predominate.

Sometimes Sandburg piles up detail, as in "Hits and Runs," and leaves the reader to absorb the mood. Such a device would be natural to a newspaper reporter. Sandburg was to exploit this technique to the utmost in later books. Chronology serves as outline in some poems (as it was to serve in his prose books)—as in "Alix," "The Year," "Memoir," and "Band Concert," which in its last line suggests teasingly more than meets the eye:

The crushed strawberries of ice cream soda places, the night
wind in cottonwoods and willows, the lattice shadows of door-
steps and porches, these know more of the story.   (*CP*, 90)

This poem is related to another pattern—the climactic, as in

"Medallion," "Crimson Rambler," and "Localities." This last poem pictures men in action over the continent, from Pennsylvania to Death Valley; and it closes with a not unexpected autumnal account of boys after walnuts, boys who have since gone to work or joined the navy or who "are not on payrolls anywhere./Their mothers are through waiting for them to come home" (*CP*, 93). The last line is built on the shock of pathos.

Besides the persistent delight in prairie sounds and sights and the ultimate though misty optimism of "Prairie," "The Four Brothers," and "Caboose Thoughts," to name only a few examples, one of the recurring motifs is that of evanescence and its concomitant death. The passing of time had been a concern to some extent in *Chicago Poems*, but in *Cornhuskers* it begins to assume a major role. The frequent autumn images contribute heavily to a sense of loss, of something gone—as in "Localities." The death note will appear now, as in this latter poem, as a concluding and startling poignancy, or again as an all-pervading element, as in "Cool Tombs."

The problem of communication still vexed the poet. In "Jabberers" (*CP*, 111) he played on the themes of the inadequacies of language and of the importance of silence even in the midst of jabbering. We reach out toward each other with words, but all around is "the night sky," the unknowable. This is the ultimate question, the query that insinuates itself on almost every page: What is beyond? The problem of dialogue, of making one's deepest self understood, was to tantalize Sandburg later. He was to tackle it in his introduction to his collection of poems for children, *Early Moon*, and in the thirty-eight "tentative" definitions of poetry which were to serve as a preface to *Good Morning, America*.

In addition to the personal references in "Prairie," Sandburg used himself as subject material elsewhere, so that *Cornhuskers* is ultimately more of a public confessional than *Chicago Poems*, in spite of the frequent use of the first person in that volume. "Wilderness" develops the theme that the poet has many traits of the animal in himself—wolf, fox, hog, fish, baboon, eagle, mockingbird; but he has much more—human qualities, a heart that "came from God-Knows-Where" and "is going to God-Knows-Where." Even here the poet could not depart from his thesis of the unknowable (*CP*, 100-1).

In "Chicago Poet" he views himself in a mirror and realizes that he is what he is without hope of change: "Liar, fool, dreamer, play-actor,/ Soldier, dusty drinker of dust—. . ." (*CP*, 101). "Interior" shows him in communion with the night. A voracious reader, he has found rich stimulation in Whitman, Rabelais, and Victor Hugo. He feels at one with all experience, including the fundamentally prairie scene which confronts him: golf links, limestone quarry, railroad yards. Over it all is the misty moonlight. Behind him are the ticking clocks. Mist, night, and the passing of time—these haunt his waking hours (*CP*, 112–13).

Cornhuskers revealed a mellowing in the poet. It turned its reader's attention away from the city toward the wide open spaces. It did not dwell so long on the idea of the folk as the stubbornly steady element. It made a return to the milieu of the poet's boyhood. But Sandburg maintained a free flow of verse established in the first book—to the chagrin of some of its readers—and he had shaped that verse, in the best poems, to enhance the meaning beyond meaning which Sandburg was fully aware is the reward for readers of all serious poetry. What was lacking chiefly was any urgency towards preserving the past as guide and teacher, as source of enrichment. Nor was there any definite program for the future, despite a persisting interest in man's present plight. In "Interior" the poet had quite clearly declared the day just past to be "so much rags," as in "Prairie" he had said that "the past is a bucket of ashes." He was demonstrating, it would seem almost callowly, no interest in much more than the next twenty-four hours. Such an attitude was odd, considering what he was to turn to in the next few years.

III *America Again*

By the autumn of 1918 it was obvious that the German Army was as good as defeated. In Scandinavia, Sandburg turned his attention almost exclusively to what was across the Baltic; Russia had revolted against the czars, and now Finland was revolting against Russia. Two men he saw a good deal of: Michael Borodin, a Russian spy ("agent") who, however, was able to give Sandburg details about current events in Russia; and Per Albin Hanson, the managing editor of the newspaper sponsored by the Social Democratic Party of Sweden. Though they might differ in many ways, Sandburg had enough in common with them as a friend of the common man to enjoy their company and, indeed, to profit by it. He tried unsuccessfully for an interview with the Swedish Crown Prince, Gustav Adolph (but would have the pleasure of talking to him forty years later). At least he had had enough variety of experience to get the flavor of his parents' country.

On his return to the United States in February, 1919, he was manager of the Chicago office of the Newspaper Enterprise Association until May. He then returned to the *Daily News,* in whose employ he remained for the next thirteen years. He was a privileged character: he could select the events he wanted to write up; he could interview the people he wanted to see. He proved so competent that city officials were content and actually pleased to have him simply telephone for their approval of his always clear and correct stories. But he also sauntered into Skid Row to talk to the men there in terms they could appreciate. He had been a hobo of sorts himself, and, when he did not know some of the current vocabulary, he could pick it up with ease.

The deliberate importing of Negroes to work more cheaply than whites stirred him to write a series on the ensuing struggle. Having collected his newspaper accounts into a single manuscript, he submitted them to Alfred Harcourt, who had recently left Holt to form the new company of Harcourt, Brace and Howe. Harcourt agreed to publish *The Chicago Race Riots, July, 1919,* with a foreword by another liberal thinker, Walter Lippmann. These articles were journalism, of course, but they were from the pen of a gifted writer, a man of deeply felt convictions. As usual, the author had concentrated on causes of the conflict as a means of arriving at resolution of the crisis. Such strategy would not be pleasing to capitalists.

A few weeks later, the managing editor of the *Daily News* appointed Sandburg motion-picture editor and arranged his schedule so that he could see five or six new films over the weekend and complete the week's assignments by Monday night. These included a special article for the Saturday edition. Under this schedule he had four or five days for his other writing. With the exception of his movie reviews and an occasional editorial, he devoted his time to poetry—and to collecting material about Abraham Lincoln, whom he had virtually worshiped since early boyhood.

During this year of 1919, he moved his family from Maywood to more spacious quarters in Elmhurst, another Chicago suburb. Not only was he doing well with the *News*, not only had Alfred Harcourt accepted his book, but he was now receiving formal recognition from his colleagues in the world of letters. In June he shared with Margaret Widdemer the Poetry Society of America Prize for 1918—for *Cornhuskers*, his second book of verse. Such acknowledgment could not help giving him assurance. He might still be controversial, his work might still be what reviewers would call "uneven," but he was undoubtedly assuming a role of leadership in America letters. Vachel Lindsay said to Harriet Monroe one day, "I don't in the least approve of free verse, but I cannot help but approve of Sandburg and Masters. I am certainly glad they are alive." [4] The Midwest was in earnest about the production of poetry.

In January, 1920, Professor Clyde Tull, chairman of the English Department at Cornell College, Mount Vernon, Iowa, offered Sandburg one hundred dollars to come out for a reading of his verse. This was the poet's first college engagement. He fell in love with Cornell College. After reciting his poems for about an hour, he brought out his guitar and began to sing some of the folk songs he had known as a boy and had been collecting ever since. His audience was delighted and totally engrossed. He went back again and again to Mount Vernon, always at the same modest fee, even after his fame had risen to its peak. (Out of generosity and first love, he even performed gratis at Cornell one night during the 1930's when money for the customary admission fee was nonexistent.) These performances were a means of increasing his income with dignity and pleasure. His experience on the lyceum circuit and in labor organization meetings was coming into use anew. From this date, he began to accept invitations for platform appearances with greater and greater frequency. Like his Midwest predecessor, James Whitcomb Riley, Sandburg was sure to find that public performances would increase the sale of his books.

CHAPTER 4

"We Are Not Sure . . ."

I *The Third Book of Verse*

IN OCTOBER, 1920, came *Smoke and Steel.* The title of the book would indicate that Sandburg had returned to the city for his material, but this was not altogether true, for such topics as "New Farm Tractor" and "Harvest Sunset" were equally predominant with urban subjects such as "Jazz Fantasia" and "An Electric Sign Goes Dark." He had dedicated his first volume of four and a half years before to Paula: "To My Wife and Pal, Lillian Steichen Sandburg." *Cornhuskers* had been for his daughters, "To Janet and Margaret." This new volume was for his brother-in-law Edward Steichen, who had been a photographer in the war and had emerged a colonel. In Steichen Sandburg felt a kindred spirit, for the dedication described him as a "painter of nocturnes and faces, camera engraver of glints and moments, listener to blue evening winds and new yellow roses, dreamer and finder, rider of great mornings in gardens, valleys, battles." Steichen, the poet has testified more than once, has been one of the great influences upon his life.

The critics,[1] for the most part, were enthusiastic about this continuation of Sandburg's poetical career—all except one or two like Arthur Wilson in *The Dial*, who thought that the "charming brute" of *Cornhuskers* was now beset with "the sententious garrulity which makes nine-tenths of Whitman impossible to any man of taste." But *The Dial* had been scathing about "Chicago" when it first appeared in *Poetry*, and Wilson was now clearly in the minority. This blow-hot, blow-cold attitude of Chicago's own *Dial* has its amusing side.

It was not that the other reviewers did not find fault. They were aware of Sandburg's vagueness as he moved off into what, for want of a better term, they called "mysticism." They also recognized his repetitiousness. They commented on his occasional reaching too far for images and on his verbosity. Amy Lowell had feared from the first that he would let propaganda destroy his art. She was of the opinion that when he wrote about "the people" his work was seldom successful. For one thing, the people who were his subjects were monotonous: there was no contrast in economic level. Whereas earlier male critics had admired his blend of vulgarity and elegance, she fastidiously objected to the outcropping of crudities that she felt marred otherwise fine poems. Especially did she find fault with his habit of dragging in a single slang word—like "stenogs" in "Trinity Place." The London *Times Literary Supplement* took issue with Sandburg's disdain of history: his slang strained too hard to be loyally contemporary; his irritation with the past too often led him to celebrate current mediocrity. Furthermore, the *Times* found him too ready to use the ugly; in fact, beauty was used only for contrast. (That this was hasty judgment a careful examination of the book will prove.)

For the most part, however, the reviewers had been won over to Sandburg at his best. He wrote too much, but a great deal of good could be distilled from his work. His custom of eliminating abstract words was paying off in powerful detail, in testimony of zest for life, in sensitiveness to shades of meaning. Though his "mysticism" was sometimes shadowy, the emotion involved was nearly always unmistakable. The familiar contrasts were still prevalent—the harsh and sinewy on the one hand and the tender and wistful on the other.

Louis Untermeyer compared and contrasted his nominations for America's two chief poets—Sandburg and Frost. (Where was E. A. Robinson?) Frost had returned from a triumph in England and was now known, like Sandburg, as the author of three books of strong poetry. Untermeyer pointed out that both poets were obviously American in temperament as well as birth. They both were a combination of gentle and rugged traits; both were attached to the earth. Furthermore, Untermeyer was impressed with their love of the simple, candid things that make up everyday life. The principal differences between the two lay in Frost's concentration and in Sandburg's comprehension: that is, whereas

Frost normally exploited a single fact without exhausting its potential, Sandburg moved over the world, fed by many facts, seeking definite answers where Frost would be content to make a subtle implication.

But *Smoke and Steel* was actually not much different from its predecessors. Like them, it was divided into titled sections: "Smoke Nights," "People Who Must," "Broken-Face Gargoyles," "Playthings of the Wind," "Mist Forms," "Accomplished Facts," "Passports," "Circles of Doors," "Haze," and "Panels." A glance at these topics shows an emphasis on the vague, the "mystical," in spite of Sandburg's acclaimed interest in daily occurrences and his emphasis on eradicating the abstract word. The two sides of Sandburg's personality were still in evidence—the "Chicago" side and the "Fog" side. The strident language of "To a Contemporary Bunkshooter" reappeared in "Galoots," "Honky Tonk in Cleveland, Ohio," and "Real Estate News." But whole sections, like "Mist Forms" and "Haze," were gentle, devoted to loveliness. (Had the London *Times* reviewer closed his eyes to these?)

Fascinated by folk music of all categories, Sandburg was very much interested in Negro music—not only in spirituals and work songs, but in blues and jazz. "Jazz Fantasia" is built on the varying moods and sounds of a small band, reflecting the vitality and emotional fervor not only of the musicians but also of their listeners. The Negro influence had made itself felt in the earlier volumes, too—in "Singing Nigger," in "Nigger," in "Potato Blossom Songs and Jigs." So this subject was nothing new.

Not new, either, was the reassertion of the poet's early devotion to the ideology of Populism. Amy Lowell wondered if he were going to end by being a mere exhorter, or if his really exquisite gift for lyric intensity would predominate and leave him with the name of poet? "The Mayor of Gary" was based on not-so-subtle descriptive contrast—the mayor himself on the one hand and the children and the working men of the steel town on the other (*CP*, 161). Materialistic greed came in for rough language in "Galoots": ". . . hunt your snacks of fat and lean, grab off yours" (*CP*, 162).

Continuing the pattern of familiarity, he even used as epigraph for "Four Preludes on Playthings of the Wind" (*CP*, 183–85) a clause from the conclusion of "Prairie": "The past is a bucket of ashes." The idea here, as usual, was that nothing is permanent except change itself. The greatest civilization in the world is doomed to eventual extinction; so why worry about either the past or the future? The best scheme is to live unthinkingly in the present. This, of course, is the way of the working classes, who are without a profound knowledge or sense of history and have no mind for or inclination towards the consolations of philosophy. Sandburg said this over and over again in poem after poem and book after book as he strove to represent a class of society of which he was no longer a member—if indeed he ever had been. Other poets have played variations on a single theme, however. What mattered was not so much what Sandburg was saying (so long as he was sincere), but with what intensity, what variety, and what originality he said it.

The title poem, "Smoke and Steel" (*CP*, 151–56), is the longest piece in the book, and the most important. It makes use both of the hard materialism at hand and of the vague mysticism which for Sandburg was never far around the corner. It is divided into ten lyric sections of unequal length, their structure growing as usual from the idea itself. The central matter is a consideration of the way men's lives are spent in the advancing of civilization through material "progress." This is not new: Thoreau was aware that railroad cars ran over the men who had built the tracks (the "sleepers"). Sandburg's way of saying it, however, had no flavor of Thoreau's somber pun. It made use, on the other hand, of a kind of mystique of the relation between steelworkers and their product, the result being an approach to mysticism which would yield a slightly different theme from the apparent one.

For example, Sandburg made much of the patterns that smoke weaves; he made a relation rise between sacrificial death and the ongoing of civilization; he moved in great variety from the frankness of "Jesus, my bones ache" to the gentle imagistic picture in "A pool of moonshine comes and waits." His words and lines varied in quality as he described the fire and smoke of the great steel mills, or the flight of an airplane through the sky, or the activity of the wind at night. The poem passes through smoke from a number of sources and through the vigor and excitement of the making of steel to a concluding silence: "The wind picks only . . . pearl cobwebs . . . pools of moonshine." Silence is all. After the fierce activity of a really energetic life, what comes but the wind, cobwebs, and the light of the moon? This, then, is the great theme of the poem. All others are mere contributing elements. Silence is all.

Of the shorter poems, many base their statement on this enigmatic reply of silence, which has haunted Sandburg all his life. "Bas-Relief" makes use of the words "mysteriously" and "mystic" in describing the flight of five wild geese. Why do they move so surely and with such dignity? The poet found no answer—except the tremendous silence that surrounds us. Bryant's waterfowl of a hundred years before had been guided by a deistic "Power," but that was over a century ago. Sandburg was not so certain. He asked the same question as did Bryant, but there he stopped. Much as he would have liked a definite answer, he heard no reply.

The same awesome quiet invests many another poem in this book. "Brass Keys" admits that there is nowhere to turn for satisfaction: ". . . there is no authority in the phone book for us to call/and ask the why, the wherefore, and the howbeit/it's . . . a riddle . . . by God" (*CP*, 181). Sandburg used ellipsis periods frequently to indicate mystery, distance, and silence.) The titles of other poems indicate this same vein: "Aprons of Silence," "Death Snips Proud Men," "And This Will Be All?"

To find happiness, however fleeting, in the things of this world is all that is left to man. "Purple Martins" develops the thesis of self-realization, of knowing oneself within the limits of one's finitude. The point is to be thoroughly oneself, simply, candidly, without hypocrisy or shame: "Be water birds, be air birds./Be these purple tumblers you are" (*CP*, 181). Had not Cully Sandburg, at the cost of sympathy and understanding from citizens of Galesburg, determined to be himself?

Of the scores of effective short poems (three lines or more), most grow out of this affirmation of life, though often a poem is only a delicate tracery of an image, touched with a mist of transience. Contrary to Amy Lowell's opinion, when slang enters a poem, it produces immediacy; sometimes, granted, it is a little shocking, but it nearly always has a subtle suggestion of poignancy coupled with a sense of the absurdity of man's plight. For example, "Eaters, go to it; your mazuma pays for it all . . ." (*CP*, 252). The human dilemma requires man to make his home in our world (as Sandburg does in relaxing into slang, in strumming a guitar, in a thousand little ways that he shows his reader), in spite of not really knowing who he is, or where he is, or above all, why he is. After the concrete details of "Balloon Faces" the poet says twice: "—this will be about all, this will be about all" (*CP*, 252). The three lines of "Mascots" end with words of sharp experience and of impermanence: "against a great hunger," "to die with," and "worth remembering" (*CP*, 264).

In many of the poems of *Smoke and Steel* Sandburg continued to use freely the clichés and hackneyed apothegms out of which his people form their conversation. These are the shibboleths, the passwords by which the common folk recognize their own kind. They are the easy, undemanding means of communication among the unreflective masses. Taken by themselves, they say little to the thoughtful reader; but their effect is cumulative. He feels after pages of these sayings that folk wisdom is indeed massive. He realizes that it has grown from a patient endurance, a basic sense of the ridiculous, and an experience of life's fundamental emotions from travail to ecstasy—on an uncomplicated level, unenriched by profundities of sophistication: it has grown from a meeting of life head on. In "Telegram" a shoemaker says, "I pay my bills, I love my wife, and I am not afraid of anybody" (*CP*, 247). "Put Off the Wedding Five Times and Nobody Comes to It" is both title, theme, and trite proverb. Several pages dotted with this familiar coin will be followed by many pages in which Sandburg's own insights and originality assume the lead. Especially free of the people's drab speech are the imagistic sections like "Mist Forms" and "Haze."

One can argue that the Imagists were working in the opposite direction, trying to head out of any mist and haze. In this respect Sandburg is related to that group but not a member of it. He has a knack for clearly etched pictures, but they are often dissipated in a cloud of uncertainty. "Night's Nothings Again" begins in silence:

> Who knows what I know
> when I have asked the night questions
> and the night has answered nothing
> only the old answers?

It moves through a cluster of evocative details, imagistic in technique, which describe New York at night. It ends with what

for Sandburg has to be a vagueness: "The hands of God wash-
ing something,/feet of God walking somewhere" (*CP* 260–63).

This somewhat agnostic attitude toward the cosmos is what
has irritated some reviewers. Not that Sandburg should possess
information that even the most devout can infer only by faith.
The irritation arises in his persistent asking of the question.
This unrelenting repetition of the unanswerable without ever
coming anywhere near a conclusion becomes tiresome, and it has
turned many discriminating readers away from the poetry of a
man who was a bold innovator in 1914.

Every poet is to some degree autobiographical. Sandburg certainly had been writing from the beginning out of his own
observation and experience. In *Smoke and Steel* he continued
to draw on the happenings of his own life. One of the poems
he called "Helga"; and another, "Winter Milk," he addressed to
Helga, for Sandburg at forty-two was now father of a third
daughter (who was herself to become a novelist).

The poems in the section headed "Passports" he had written
at the time he had gone to Stockholm in the winter of 1918–19.
One can follow his progress—Washington, New York, the
Atlantic, Stockholm, Christiania, and the Baltic. The tone is a
familiar one: loving detail of observation, but a pervading loneliness, here channeled into a longing for Illinois. Fairly grave,
these poems are lighted by very little humor, show a characteristic awareness of man's plight on the part of the author, and
yet are highly affirmative. Appreciation of the sensuous surface
is here, as everywhere in Sandburg, but it is supported by the
realization—on the part of the characters or the poet himself as
participant and observer—that man is trapped in a cage of
unknowing.

Of the three lines of "Fog Portrait" (*CP*, 235–36) each ends
with the phrase: "a woman's steel face . . . looking . . . looking." (Here are the ellipsis periods again.) "In the Shadow of
the Palace" concludes with a hortatory "Let us go out in the
fog, John. . ." (*CP*, 237). Sandburg had been asking the same
cosmic question from the beginning: at the Yeats dinner in 1914
he had read "Limited," in which he asks a fellow passenger
where he is going and receives the pragmatic reply, "Omaha."
The conclusion must be that the people, Sandburg's people, are
too ignorant, too fatigued, or too indifferent to make the query.

Nearly always it was Sandburg who was asking the question of them (without, of course, finding the answer). When one gets down to it, "Omaha" may well be the wise answer for the common man. What good are abstractions, T. S. Eliot's "hints and guesses," except to philosophers?

To try analysis of all the poems in *Smoke and Steel* would be futile and tiresome. Two of the pieces (one must pick and choose) deserve attention. Whereas Vachel Lindsay's "General William Booth Enters Heaven" pictures a county-seat with sweetly transforming evangelism and a promise of eternal happiness for repentant sinners, Sandburg's "The Sins of Kalamazoo" admits to evil, but nothing as scarlet as Lindsay's lyric tale rather gently describes. Mediocrity and indifference walk the streets of Kalamazoo. (In another poem, "My People," Sandburg said his "people are gray," [*CP*, 266].) Its citizens marry, work, and go to town on Saturday night. In the *persona* of a "loafer," Sandburg strolls through the streets and characteristically wonders what all these daily activities mean. He loves the way of life in Kalamazoo, but he finds no reason for it—no answer except "a fadeaway," for both he and the town will disappear. He feels ultimately only the old uncertainty—"a creeping mystic what-is-it" (*CP*, 175).

The book concludes with a benediction poem, a prayer for peace, "For You." The twelve three-line stanzas are generally parallel in structure, the three- and four-stress lines contributing to the steadying mood. The opening is a metaphor—doors leading to great experiences, whether made by man (churches and libraries) or by nature (prairies, seas, and mountains). The poet would hope for "you" the knowledge of and appreciation for people of heroic mold, memories of great personages. But with memory one realizes the inevitable—that all must change, though this fact may be made affirmative by a joy in promise and development (the future belongs to the presently playful young):

> The peace of great changes be for you.
> Whisper, Oh beginners in the hills.
> Tumble, Oh cubs—tomorrow belongs to you.
> (*CP*, 268)

Through all vicissitudes, a full life requires and should cling to love, for it is in the dialogue of love that life becomes the radiant experience. Finally, emulating Whitman ("Very well then I contradict myself"), Sandburg hopes "you" will have a sense of the past, a feeling of belonging, of heritage. Though all must pass, memory is inescapable; so one might do well to affirm it after all. History may be only "a bucket of ashes" at one place in Sandburg's pages, but he concluded *Smoke and Steel* with the note that at least a vague contact with the past makes one's present life more fruitful.

❊   ❊   ❊

The London *Times Literary Supplement*, though finding *Smoke and Steel* dominated by an almost reckless determination to be American, conceded nevertheless that the energy in the lines was impressive and that the poems were successful in attaining what they had set out to accomplish. The British reviewer ended by echoing the question of many of Sandburg's readers: Did these poems rightfully deserve to be called art in the best sense?

Edmund Wilson emphatically said "no." Very soon after the publication of *Smoke and Steel* he published an essay in *Vanity Fair*[2] in which he asserted that the industrial revolution had dulled the sensibilities of America's poets. Among the others, Sandburg could not communicate emotional reactions and had resorted to colorless diction; he was, in short, totally lacking in taste. Wilson was careful to say that the poets were the victims of their time, but they nevertheless were "The Anarchists of Taste." Sandburg was angered by this blast. He had many friends and supporters, but he was vexed that a critic would not see what was happening in the world of letters, would not see that a breakthrough was necessary to avoid stagnation and death.

He made some explanation of what he and his fellows were about. He told Walter Yust of *The Bookman*[3] that he and the other experimenters were trying to achieve "a kind of freedom. We are not sure we are writing poetry. Remember Nora in Ibsen's 'Doll's House'? She fought for something—a miracle she called it. She didn't know what it would be like, but she knew it was something fine, and that she had to go after it. That's the way we're moving along. I guess really we don't know where we're going, but we're on our way. We may never win this freedom; maybe we'll be interesting to future generations only because we are a step toward a higher development. I don't know."

Sandburg's early critics had questioned the poetic quality of some of his pieces. Now he was willing to accept their skepticism, though with complete faith in what he was doing. One remembers here what Yeats had said in 1914 of the trend toward humility—and toward vivid imagery. One must conclude that Sandburg was himself humble about his work. He felt that he was writing what he must, but whether he was turning out the real thing he would not venture to say. (Had he been talking to Harriet Monroe? "Whether you call it poetry or not," she had said of his first book.)

He went on to say to his interviewer that young poets who had taken to writing "this new human, racy, vigorous verse . . . want the truth, . . . and they want to share what they find of it, honestly, . . . with hard, unequivocal picture-words." And then he discussed his own working habits. "I cut out all words ending in *ity* and *ness* as far as I can. That is, I cut out words describing 'state of being.' And I search for picture-words, as the Indians have them, as the Chinese have them." It was not easy for him to write a poem. He expended a great deal of time and energy—often a month or more—in looking for the right words and in polishing his structures. He confessed that the version of "Prairie" that had finally come to print in *Cornhuskers* had been the fourteenth. So if Edmund Wilson had the impression that Sandburg was not a fastidious craftsman, he was mistaken. Maybe Sandburg did not arrive at results pleasing to Wilson, but as a poet he chose his words and ordered them with great care. And he was being read—widely—by people of taste.

Sandburg's admiration for Whitman was now a nationally known fact. Boni and Liveright had asked him early in 1920 to write an introduction to the Modern Library edition of *Leaves of Grass*. In May, one of the editors had to write him asking that he make some changes in his essay. His prose style was influenced by his assimilation of hobo and street-corner slang and needed to be somewhat modified! But the book came out in 1921, Sandburg warning its readers that "it is impossible for a poet to tell you anything worth knowing unless you already know it. . ." [4]. Did he feel that Edmund Wilson, for example, lacked that necessary foreknowledge?

II   *A Book for Helga*

Sandburg had dedicated books to Paula, to his two older daughters, to his brother-in-law. The 1922 volume was for Helga, the baby. Sandburg was deeply devoted to his family. Dedication of his books was one way of showing how he felt.

Slabs of the Sunburnt West is a misleading name for this book. Bringing the volume to its close, the title poem, which is about the Grand Canyon, is the only piece about the far West. The rest of the poems are concerned, as usual, with Chicago, Washington, the sea, and the prairie. Furthermore, this final poem is not so strong and intense as some of the others, notably "Windy City," the longest and the most deeply felt piece in the volume.

Sandburg's techniques were the same as they had been in 1914. He was no longer a revolutionist in prosody and language, for his revolt had now become habit and had lost its novelty. Sandburg had in his beginnings elbowed out John G. Neihardt, George Sterling, and Madison Cawein. Now he was giving way to a new generation; he belonged to the status quo; he was himself an old boy. It is significant that Malcolm Cowley's largely sympathetic review of *Slabs of the Sunburnt West* appeared in the same issue of *The Dial* as the first momentous publication of T. S. Eliot's *The Waste Land*. The tide had turned.

Cowley was especially impressed with Sandburg's diction. In contrast with H. L. Mencken's scholarly and objective interest in the American language, Sandburg "never wrote an American dictionary, but he does something more hazardous and exciting: he writes American." [5] Raymond Holden, in *The New Republic*, though admiring Sandburg's "personality, genius, perspicacity, fire, love of life," was of the opinion that his "vernacular beauty" was "often effaced by his fear that dignity will estrange it." Likewise, Arthur Guiterman in *The Independent* resented "the special brand of thieves' slang or local and temporary argot that happens to strike his momentary fancy." The New York *Times* reviewer feared that Sandburg had espoused a bad habit: he was "in danger of becoming the Professional Chanter of Virility."

But the reviewer admitted that nearly all the shorter (and quieter) poems were successful, a result attributable to the fact that Sandburg was best when conveying moods, which after all did not last very long at a time and warranted brief verses.

Sandburg had been Harriet Monroe's discovery. She was still loyal, but in her review she singled out only five poems for commendation. "The Windy City" and "Washington Monument by Night" were to her the best; "At the Gates of Tombs" provided humor both sad and grotesque; and "Primer Lesson" and "Harsk, Harsk" were good for one or two readings. She was sorry that the organization of the rest of the poems was not tighter, more coherent. Her opinion of the title poem was that its author was obviously more a part of Chicago than he was of the Grand Canyon and hence could not write of that phenomenon with the same intensity of feeling that he had for his home city. "The Windy City" was clearly Miss Monroe's favorite. She found in it more plan and shape than in earlier poems of similar length. She also felt in it a power and a splendor that fulfilled her faith in Sandburg. Whereas "Chicago" had been an etching made up of a few bold lines, "The Windy City" was a great picture, complex and brilliantly colored.

The poem is divided into ten sections, the first delineating the city's origin, the second showing an easy-going acceptance of its history (no special "feeling" for the past). At the third section a shift to choppy rhythms changes the mood. Sandburg here lists a series of popular sayings like "You said a mouthful" and "Bring home the bacon." He calls this process "jazz[ing] the classics"—putting the basic themes into the vernacular. This catalogue was a foreshadowing of the even more elaborate enchiridions in *Good Morning, America* and *The People, Yes,* but it was also a remnant of the banging and shouting of his earlier work.

In the fourth section the poet tries to place Chicago among the world's cities and finds its distinguishing characteristic to be its utter independence: it is like "a hog on ice," a motif first suggested in "Chicago." More specifically then in the next two sections, he points out the two most salient traits of the city's life: its monotony, misery, and pitiful attempts at imaginative living; and the tremendous energy expended in tearing down and building up in never-ceasing cycle. Whitman's lilacs have become in Sandburg symbols of desire for beauty in the face of destructive industrialism, but now even the lilacs have gone.

> And dooryard lilacs near a malleable iron works
> Long ago languished
> In a short whispering purple.
>
> (CP, 275)

For the other theme he turns to his Socialist-Populist sympathies: it is the people who make the city; they are proud of its material wealth in their own way, for they are responsible for the building and the maintaining of the skyscrapers: "Put the city up; tear the city down;/put it up again; let us find a city" (CP, 277). Sandburg had also put this restless energy into his earliest poems. Almost parallel in image had been one of the "War Poems (1914–1915)" called "And They Obey" (CP, 40). The people may not have the imagination or the enterprise for leadership, but they are the foundations of the world's work.

As "The Windy City" draws to its close, Sandburg paints in the dots and spots of illumination in the metropolis at night, an aspect he had enjoyed from the beginning ("Night Movement—New York," "Sunset from Omaha Hotel Window"). The final or tenth section turns its attention to the winds that give the city its nickname. As they blow in the four seasons, they bring both plenty and hardship. A favorite theme rises from this paean: nature goes on, though cities rise and fall. The last four lines are a repetition of lines in the sixth section:

> The wind of the lake shore waits and wanders.
> The heave of the shore wind hunches the sand piles.
> The winkers of the morning stars count out cities
> And forget the numbers.
>
> (CP, 282)

The nine divisions of "Washington Monument by Night" are very short. The poem is built on the tension of contrast between the suffering and bickering during the American Revolution (especially at Valley Forge) and the sturdiness of General Washington at the center of things. The ninth section is composed of two lines, each made up of three sets of ellipsis periods. What is the idea? Was Sandburg struck silent in gratitude and admiration? At any rate, the poem trails off into silence, that ever-present nothing that surrounds all.

Opinions varied on "And So Today" (*CP*, 283–88), another of the long poems. Miss Monroe, who would be fair if anyone would, could find nothing new either in what it said or in the way it said it. The New York *Times*, on the other hand, picked it as the best poem in the book.

The subject matter of the poem is the burial of the Unknown Soldier in Arlington. The fanfare, the procession, the pomp and ceremony are tempered by a horse laugh. The beauty of the roses becomes ironical in juxtaposition to the slang and the cynicism. In "To a Contemporary Bunkshooter" Sandburg had yelled back at the evangelist in the wildest kind of anger. In "And So Today" he was using the same language, but less aggressively; the tone was not so much angry as bitterly objective. Comments of the reporters who will write up the event for their newspapers cut through the hypocrisy of the ritual: "Moonshine," "bull . . . bull . . . bull," "Hokum." Over all hovers the theme of futility, for Sandburg sees the riders in the procession as "skeleton riders on skeleton horses," and he asks the "stars of the night sky" whether they have seen them (for men are ephemeral, even if the flow of the people seems eternal). The boy is buried "with music and roses—under a flag—/under a sky of promises." The final effect is bitter and ironical; Sandburg sees no good in war, but can propose no alternative. His question: After all, the boy is dead; so what's the point?

The remaining long poem, "Slabs of the Sunburnt West" (*CP*, 307–14), is in three parts. The first evokes the night journey by train to the Grand Canyon. It reflects on the region's past, the inscrutable quality of the desert. Meanwhile, in the club car, cigar-smoking men bandy about the words "civilizations," "history," "God," cliché-ridden time-killers in the face of the silent and waiting expanses through which the men are traveling. One remembers the patient waiting of nature in "Prairie," and he is also reminded of the trivial conversation about Michelangelo at the party J. Alfred Prufrock attends.

The second part of "Slabs of the Sunburnt West" is the longest. It is a record of impressions of the Grand Canyon itself as seen from the back of a donkey, surefooted in negotiating the precipices. Inevitably Sandburg is led to ask the big questions, for he realizes that he knows nothing of the universes beyond the stars. The experience brings home to him the ultimate absurdity of man's situation. Man has only his five senses, and they cannot begin to answer his questions. All they can say is "Wait."

Sandburg resorts to rugged humor. The walls of the canyon suggest a great variety of figures to the observer. As the sun goes down, the shadows suggest a game of baseball, but "the game is called on account of darkness." This is the metaphor at the base of all his poetry. Supporting the idea of man's finitude and the continuance of the life principle itself is a childlike refrain that occurs four times in the section:

> A bluejay blue
> and a gray mouse gray
> ran up the canyon walls.

In the midst of all this grandeur, against a background of august creation, life goes on, however insignificant.

The last part of the poem is a brief coda. Night has fallen. The answer to the question is typically ambiguous: burning-out stars forecast early death; vigorous, brilliant stars prophesy long life; "runaway stars" (meteors? comets?) promise escape into eternal life. Little man's query receives no reliable response; the uncertainty remains: is he doomed to die—or not?

The short poems in the book follow the same patterns as Sandburg's earlier work. Mist, dusk, fog, smoke—all play their equivocal, almost conspiratorial part. A few genre pieces accent the landscape. "Gypsy Mother" describes a woman on Halsted Street:

> A red shawl on her shoulders falls with a fringe hem to a green
>   skirt;
> Chains of yellow beads sweep from her neck to her tawny hands.
> Fifty springtimes must have kissed her mouth holding a calabash
>   pipe.
>
> (CP, 295)

"At the Gates of Tombs" has a familiar conclusion: "And since at the gates of tombs silence is a gift,/be silent about it, yes, be silent—forget it" (CP, 294). The last two words have the ring of the colloquial, almost of bravado in the face of the awful inevitable.

Slabs of the Sunburnt West was on the whole a mellower, quieter volume than any of the others. Though the New York

Times objected to what it thought was a forced and artificial virility in some passages (possibly in this very "At the Gates of Tombs"), the over-all tone of this collection was subdued; and the vernacular, the sudden slang, the boisterous humor were all employed with care. A principal objection would have to be the monotony of theme.

CHAPTER 5

Lincoln and America

I *The Prairie Years*

SANDBURG'S FIRST BOOK of tales for children, *Rootabaga Stories,* was to be published in mid-November, 1922. These were a writing-down of fantastic narratives he had improvised for his daughters. He wrote in October to Harcourt asking him the favor of an advance on royalties on the forthcoming volume, for he wanted to buy the lot next door in Elmhurst to insure not only privacy (which was now hard to come by), but playing space for his three daughters. He was proving to be valuable property to his publishers and could make such requests with all confidence.

Sandburg's books and platform performances were making him well-known and well-liked. In 1923 he was invited to participate in the celebration of the fiftieth anniversary of the Chicago Public Library. He obliged by making a little speech and reading some of his poems. In this year too, his friend Harry Hansen devoted seventy-five pages to him in *Midwest Portraits,* in an informal sketch in which he described Carl's workroom in Elmhurst and quoted him on the subject of his years spent in Galesburg and on the road.

Rootabaga Stories sold so well that Harcourt brought out another set of tales, *Rootabaga Pigeons,* in the fall. This second collection was such a success that Harcourt asked Sandburg to come to New York to discuss still a third children's book. But the lovely nonsense of the Rootabaga world had been incidental to Sandburg. For several years he had been accumulating Lincoln lore, and by this time he was almost totally absorbed by the adventure of tracking down, cataloguing, and recording his materials. His focus was on Lincoln as a prairie figure, one of his own sort. He had devised an elaborate, if eccentric, filing system and was collecting data from every possible source. So Sandburg told Harcourt that, if he would let him write about Lincoln, he would be happy to submit an outline for a children's biography of about four hundred pages. Harcourt was interested. Sandburg went home and submerged himself in his new task.

The Chicago of the 1920's was an exciting and stimulating place to be. On the *Daily News* staff alone men and women were turning out numerous books of poetry, fiction, criticism, and biography, as well as studies of the social scene and of government. Ben Hecht, for one, was a prolific contributor to journals of all sorts. In 1928 he and Charles MacArthur produced their astounding newspaper play, *The Front Page*, on Broadway. Edna Ferber, who had gone to New York, came back to the shores of Lake Michigan to stay for weeks as she worked on a novel. Sherwood Anderson had just finished *Winesburg, Ohio,* and was exploring the possibilities of the novel. Margaret Ayer Barnes was there, and Mary Hastings Bradley. Books were coming from Clarence Darrow, from Jane Addams, from George Barr McCutcheon, whose brother, John T. McCutcheon, was drawing brilliant cartoons for the Chicago *Tribune.* Booth Tarkington and Meredith Nicholson often came from Indianapolis for glorious visits. Another Hoosier, George Ade, often joined them from his farm in Newton County.

Magazines were numerous: *The Red Book, The Blue Book, The Green Book, College Humor,* *Women's World.* Experimental theaters welcomed the work of untried playwrights. Hull House Players was giving Paul Muni a start. Artists of all kinds and degrees abounded, and the Art Institute was a dominant influence. Covici-McGee-Booksellers on Washington Street was a popular gathering place for writers: Masters, Anderson, Darrow, Hecht, MacArthur, Vincent Sheean, and John Gunther went there to browse, to talk books, and to speculate about life with their friends.

Sandburg mingled with these people. He saw a good deal of Harriet Monroe. As he walked the streets alone, he found in the slums, the Loop, the lake more subject matter than his pen could do justice to. As he explored the subject of Abraham Lincoln, he found friends outside the newspaper and literary circles, including Oliver R. Barrett, a wealthy lawyer who had a fine collection of Lincoln materials. He lunched and dined with his colleagues at the Cheesebox, at Schlogl's Restaurant, at the Dill Pickle. He sometimes stayed late at his *Daily News* desk to polish a poem and then caught a late train to Elmhurst.

All the while he was learning about Lincoln, trying to clear up the sentimental view and to make real this man who had become a legendary figure of colossal proportions. He accepted platform engagements in cities and towns where he knew he could learn something more about his hero. After a performance he would remain a day or two to talk to people who had known the man or to copy letters and other relevant documents. At last, after more than two years of hard but exciting work, the Lincoln manuscript was ready. Alfred Harcourt talked the editor of the *Pictorial Review* into running a section of the book as a serial. The price was $27,500. This was big money.

Abraham Lincoln: The Prairie Years was published in two volumes in February, 1926, celebrating its subject's one-hundred-twenty-fifth birthday. The nuances, the complexities, and the consequent length had gone beyond the expectation of either Harcourt or Sandburg. What had started as a four-hundred-page project for children was now nine hundred pages addressed to grown-ups. The narrative begins in 1776. It ends as Lincoln is leaving Springfield for his inauguration in Washington. Kentucky, southern Indiana, central Illinois—Sandburg followed the man every step of the way; and wherever the next step was shadowy he speculated, sometimes in a kind of free-verse fantasy. It is this exercise of invention that Edmund Wilson disliked,[1] for Sandburg had practiced poetic license in a genre that requires the strictest adherence to fact.

The new biography brought a shower of praise from reviewers. They found flaws in the factual accounts, they winced sometimes at the too-elaborate embroideries in the development of evidence, they were sometimes confused by the non-selectivity of materials. But almost to a man they admitted that the author had created a portrait of a man, a myth of a hero, and a panorama of a maturing nation through his presentation of sheer massed detail.

As Sandburg had at first planned his work as a book for young people, so indeed two years later the first twenty-six chapters were reissued for just such an audience with the title (taken *verbatim* from Chapter 12) *Abe Lincoln Grows Up*, an account which stops at the family's move from Indiana to Illinois. Though scholarly critics found omissions and errors, these chapters were nevertheless crammed with facts that interested children. There was no denying it, Sandburg had a thoroughgoing familiarity with his data. Not only had he been diligently gathering information from every possible source for many years, but he had been absorbing it, making it his own; now he had given it to the world colored by his own personality.

As factual history, then, *The Prairie Years* was overwhelmingly loaded. The author frequently used the fairly obvious device of cataloguing. So rich was his store of data and myths that he was often carried away by the piles of detail; like Whitman before him, he reveled in the names of things. These frequent lists gave a kind of concreteness to the narrative; they had the advantage that in quick succession they brought to the mind of the reader myriad images that made the larger action of history come alive. Similarly, brief incidents were stacked one on another quickly and sometimes without much immediately evident coherence, but the total effect was convincing for most of his readers. The times, the country, and the man were of such a complex nature that this method of accumulation was appropriate to the subject.

If on the one side Sandburg seemed all-inclusive, he at the same time, especially in the earlier chapters, omitted general details that might have painted more realistically a background crude and raw. Following in this instance a romantic tradition, Sandburg selected his material in such a way that the end result was the truth as he saw it, but not the whole truth. Most of his 1926 readers, though, felt that, despite his errors of omission and commission, he had given the world an appropriate biography of Lincoln. Even the lack of footnotes bothered few critics at the time, for scholarly industry was obvious without such pedantry. Sandburg was not out to settle disputed points; he was not trying to introduce much new information. He was creating—or rather, solidifying—an American myth; he was not writing history for schoolroom and study.

As for the errors this sprawling book contained, later condensations and excerpted editions (notably the one-volume edition of

1954) corrected many of them. In this first edition, however, Sandburg referred to the early tradition that the Lincolns had had neither cow nor horse when they had moved from Kentucky into Indiana, whereas scholars had proved that they had had horses and that they must have had cows in order to contract "milk sick." In one of the early imaginative chapters—which Edmund Wilson refers to as "corn," for who could tell exactly what happened?—Sandburg portrayed Nancy Hanks on her death bed and speaking to her two children: "A bony hand of the struggling mother went out, putting its fingers into the boy's sandy black hair; her fluttering guttural words seemed to say he must grow up and be good to his sister and father" (*Ch.* 11). Sandburg also understated the cost of the Mexican War; moreover, he called John Quincy Adams "a sweet, lovable man," testimony that those who knew him could not have accepted.

Sandburg also placed Crawfordsville, Indiana, on the Wabash River (maybe confused by the fact that Crawfordsville is the seat of Wabash College); he said that Shelley had drowned in an Italian lake rather than in the Gulf of Spezzia; and he quoted de Tocqueville but gave credit to Montesquieu. When he made use of a letter of Lincoln's to Mrs. Lincoln, he claimed that it had never before been published, but one diligent scholar found it in a 1904 edition of Lincoln letters.[2] But rare indeed is the work of even the most cautious professional historian—documentation and all—without its factual mistakes. In view of the final effect of *The Prairie Years* on its readers, the listing of errors may seem petty.

What Sandburg accomplished in his famous biography was the presentation of Lincoln in the years before he went to the White House against an elaborate backdrop of his environment—not only the problems of pioneer settlements but the larger changes taking place in agriculture, industry, and economics. Except for Sandburg's imaginative flights when facts were missing, the author scarcely ever departed from the anecdotal into interpretation or to present insights. He nevertheless gave the effect of social, political, and national forces at work, of the great westward movement, of the evolving consciousness in the plain folk of their political destiny. He used a quick and vivid pen in describing the Mexican War, the war in Kansas, the

CARL SANDBURG

Lincoln-Douglas debates, the place of Harriet Beecher Stowe, of John Brown, of Dred Scott—all to show the inevitable drive toward the Civil War. But his organization and technique, being diurnal, never permitted him to look ahead, to evaluate in the light of coming events. Of Mrs. Stowe, he wrote: "By the device of dramatizing a black Christ, she led millions of people to believe there were two countries with two cultures in the United States; in one humanity was desecrated; in the other it was held sacred" (Ch. 90). This sentence described the actual situation; Sandburg added no comment.

Out of the great welter of fact and imagination emerged a man, a hero, a myth. Sandburg showed Lincoln as the product of his rural-village environment and his character as built on tensions resulting from some humanizing weaknesses and from some out-of-the-ordinary powers. The distinctive qualities in Lincoln, as Sandburg saw them, were his earthiness and at the same time his undeniable loftiness of spirit, both enveloped in an inexplicable mystery. Through the slow accretion of fact and incident, the biographer showed the development of an awkward, though gregarious boy without formal education into a statesman who, though god-like by the poet's implication, remained simple and natural to the end of the story.

Although Sandburg admitted that this prairie boy had sprung from good stock—Virginia gentry, Pennsylvania Quakers, Massachusetts Puritans—Lincoln is viewed as a product of environment, not of heredity. ("The past is a bucket of ashes.") Because of the inaccessibility of schools and because of poverty, Lincoln educated himself under what would have been insurmountable difficulties for men of lesser character. He absorbed Aesop, Bunyan, the Bible; he wrote verse; he studied Daniel Webster's orations and analyzed the sources of their brilliance. But he also enjoyed daily contact with the people around him. He joined clubs that sought earnestly after a breadth of culture and a refinement of the senses. At the same time, he enjoyed exchanging shady stories with the rest of the men. He paid court; he fell in love. Companionable, sociable though he was, he was also paradoxically sad, melancholy, and lonely. He yearned for distinction; he nurtured a sense of ambition.

What Sandburg did in this book was to depict a young man who was sometimes a clown, sometimes a philosopher; he was at the same time almost primeval and yet sophisticated—wise, humane, aware. If he was a solitary man, Lincoln could not be presented as desolate. His melancholy grew from a profound, indefinable identification with man's fate, a pensiveness tempered by quiet bravery and loving insight. But Sandburg did not hesitate to draw harsh lines of Lincoln as the pragmatic lawyer and as the opportunistic politician. Though he was intellectually honest, though his principles were undeniably firm, Lincoln was at the same time shrewd and enterprising. His point of view, though built on the Jeffersonian tradition that was the contemporary faith of nearly all of America in the first half of the nineteenth century, was essentially a conservative stand. Though he believed in an essentially rural economy and in equality of opportunity, for him the answer to the security of the country lay in a reasonably high tariff, in solid banking, and in America-first improvements. Despite his humble beginnings he was not a member of the proletariat.

As the second volume draws to a close, Lincoln's character becomes clear. His obscurity-to-fame story is at base in the American tradition, to the point of being a cliché, but as Sandburg told it, it was overwhelming in supporting detail—a repository for nearly all available materials. At the end of his years on the prairie, Lincoln stood for universal freedom, for democracy as demonstrated in the Union, for liberty, for law and order. Though rough-hewn and apparently simple, he had a nobility of spirit that lifted him above the common mass. He had soul. He knew the immensity of the responsibility awaiting him in the nation's capital: "I go to assume a task more difficult than that which devolved upon General Washington." The Englishman Leonard Woolf saw Sandburg's concept of Lincoln as the reversal of the biblical scapegoat: the world's guilt and obtuseness were about to be borne by one who was emerging *from* the wilderness.[3]

Using thousands of facts, Sandburg created a portrait of Lincoln at the same time simple and complex. The key to his method and purpose may be found in a sentence in the Preface: "The folk-lore Lincoln, the maker of stories, the stalking and elusive Lincoln is a challenge for any artist." The author intended to use the facts—but also the lore that had accumulated—to attain the flavor of the subject. Lincoln was both plain and complex; he was both of the people and removed from them.

The chapters in the book are very short, and this brevity itself may have the psychological result of inviting the reader to go further at a sitting than longer, more complicated divisions might. Each chapter also ends in such a way as to lead the reader into the next one, which in turn has an engaging beginning. Chapter 113 ends with this sentence: "There were times when Abraham Lincoln himself seemed to be a sort of ghost standing on a platform in broad daylight before thousands of people solemnly unwrapping the sheets about their old laws and murmuring of forgotten oaths and wasted sacrifices." The next chapter begins: "On an Illinois Central Railroad train of special coaches, with a brass cannon on a flat car at the rear, Stephen A. Douglas campaigned downstate." Vivid images, up-beat beginnings—these were the work of a calculating, conscious craftsman. They offer a combination of colorful detail and of imaginative metaphor. The narrative has the effect of a novel rather than of objective, factual history. Episodic rather than continual, the rapid succession of brief accounts produces a complete, panoramic, elaborate work, constantly shifting but finally quite clear. Realism is interrupted by poetic rhapsody, especially in the material about the early years, concerning which the facts are often obscure or even irrecoverable. For example, in Chapter 12, the Lincoln family having moved to Little Pigeon Creek in Indiana, Sandburg in a one-paragraph metaphor developed, through an objective correlative, a sense of young Abe's maturing.

Ten years pass and the roots of a tree spread out finding water to carry up to branches and leaves that are in the sun; the tree thickens, the forked limbs shine wider in the sun; they pray with their leaves in the rain and the whining wind; the tree arrives, the mystery of its coming, spreading, growing, a secret not even known to the tree itself; it stands with its arms stretched to the corners the four winds come from, with its murmured testimony, "We are here, we arrived, roots are in the earth of these years," and beyond that short declaration, it speaks nothing of the decrees, fates, accidents, destinies, that made it an apparition of its particular moment.

Such a figure owes much to Sandburg's interest in primitives, in the unsophisticated affirmations of the people which he had woven into his poems.

Even if Sandburg had not written books of verse that met with acclaim, one would have to conclude that *The Prairie Years* is the work of a writer with the poet's feeling and often the poet's eye. Every once in a while Sandburg may have strained his imagination to find a fresh simile, as when he likened Lincoln's gentleness and tenderness to violets. Some passages may have struck critics such as Edmund Wilson as "corny." For the taste of some readers his sense of proportion is occasionally off balance: some material may actually be irrelevant or given more attention than it deserves; for some readers the "poetic" passages may get in the way not only of the movement but of the growing image of the subject; in avoiding muckraking, Sandburg may have romanticized his material by omitting descriptions of actual crude, raw situations, especially in the early chapters—the accounts of Lincoln's boyhood. The rhapsodizing—about Lucy and Nancy Hanks or about the Ann Rutledge romance—may irritate some readers. At one point, in writing of Lincoln's letters to his father, which show a real ugliness of feeling between the two men, Sandburg, without making a romantic falsehood of his story, nevertheless withdrew behind some imaginative language that evaded the penetrating truth (Chapter 75).

If one says that Sandburg was no muckraker, he is not at the same time saying that the biographer was incapable of realism, for he recognized that his pioneer characters had flaws—jealousies, crudities, prejudices; but he held these weaknesses in balance while he sought for, and found, commendable traits that in the long run offset the sins and foibles. By and large, Sandburg was faithful to his people and their surroundings; he tried for a fair accounting. For example, the wisdom of the folk, distilled into "sayings," he recorded word for word, as he was doing in his poetry: "If the sun shines while it is raining, it will rain again the next day; birds and hens singing during the rain indicate fair weather; if roosters crow when they go to roost it is a sign of rain. . . ." He had listed similar proverbs in *Slabs of the Sunburnt West* and was to continue the practice in later books. One way of conveying the emotions and the vicissitudes of the people, he was firmly convinced, was to list the mottoes they lived by.

The forthright cataloguing of folk-wisdom is at one end of Sandburg's spectrum of style. The poetic license to which some critics object is at the other. On the whole, however, if the reader does not take these flights of fancy too hard (and certainly not literally), the interpretations, the imagery, and even the extravagant tangents add up to a contribution to the truth as Sandburg saw it. Written by a storyteller and a poet, his book was in the end making a bid, not as history or biography, but as literature. The way he looked at the ante-bellum era did not add to historical knowledge, but it did urge the reader to exercise his imagination in a way that genuine literature must inevitably do. One must return to the judgment that the end result was good.

His style is simple enough that quite a young and unsophisticated person can understand and enjoy the biography. At the same time, the very mountain of material gives the total work tremendous complexity. Sandburg had been simple and direct, had not ground any axes, had not used his material for his own aggrandizement; he had been, in a word, Yeats's vivid, modest poet. He told one interviewer: "I wanted to take Lincoln away from the religious bigots and the professional politicians and restore him to the common people." [4] This purpose he had achieved as far as simplicity and honesty went. Most of the first reviewers found the book "delightful," "sparkling," "striking," "beautiful," "exquisite." Almost all agreed that this was virtually a book of poetry—Sandburg's best poem to date—its speech characterized by the slow drawl of his native Midwest, its diction depending alike on the pithiness of every day and on the exalted vocabulary of the bard. Almost without a dissenting phrase, these first readers testified to the glow, the vividness, the vitality of the two volumes. Writing out of the deepest affection for his hero, he was writing with conviction, passion, and energy. His reverence and devotion were tempered by his honesty and common sense. He made no attempt to psychoanalyze Lincoln but, in general, simply to present the outward facts, colored though they were, particularly at the beginning, with a poetic infusion. As a matter of truth, as the volumes progressed and

Lincoln was shown to be maturing, Sandburg more and more discarded the technique of misty, metaphorical rhapsodizing and delineated Lincoln and his milieu more plainly. The fuller records of Lincoln's later years had much to do with this shift.

The London *Times Literary Supplement* [5] was grateful to Sandburg. Englishmen always appear to be baffled by the intricacies of the American political system: "It says much for Mr. Sandburg's clarity of thought and expression that he makes us see American politics almost intelligibly. Again and again we watch Lincoln bring forth his meditations to the light through great struggle." If the English found the book ultimately clear, the piling up of detail must have shown direction and purpose.

The Prairie Years, in spite of its many shortcomings as history, biography, and imaginative literature, has a universality built of thousands of particularities. It proves that prairie society was not special, but typical of pioneers anywhere on the continent; for most of the United States was still rural, its people all one people. At the same time it paints Lincoln in the glory that was his own. In general Sandburg avoided the hackneyed phrase and made his book tender, reverent, but honest in its showing forth of praise. At the same time he had seen to it that Lincoln stayed alive throughout as man, hero, myth.

II *Good Morning, America*

With the first royalties from the new biography the Sandburgs bought a summer house on Lake Michigan in the midst of a seven-acre sandy plot south of Benton Harbor at Harbert. They began spending their summers there to enjoy the change and to escape, during school vacations, from the visits of parties of children who wanted to see the author of "Fog." Sandburg continued his work for the *Daily News* at seventy-five dollars a week; for, after all, he had developed into a journalist, he had made many friends through newspaper work, and the job gave him sufficient leisure to pursue his other interests.

In the early fall of 1926 Rebecca West in London published an edition of some of his poems to introduce them to the British public. Though a large part of her introduction was devoted to an impression of Chicago as a phenomenon, she did conclude that "Carl Sandburg expresses the whole life of the Middle West of to-day." She would not have had unanimous support from American critics in this assessment, for some of them thought that Sandburg's view was limited by his ideology. But her book served an important cause in bringing American literature to a rather circumspect but potentially curious foreign audience.

On December 30, while he was in Santa Fe, Carl received a telegram from his brother Martin saying that their mother had died in Galesburg. As he returned for the funeral, he reflected that she had not worked in vain, for her children were realizing the potentials of America and were doing well. August Sandburg had died in 1910, too soon to see what his children might come to, but Clara had been able to take pleasure in watching America reward their struggles. Offspring of peasants, they could not have risen so high in Europe. Carl himself had dedicated *The Prairie Years* to his parents, "Workers on the Illinois Prairie." Sturdy stock had borne sound fruit, and the poet was proud of his origins.

In this year, too, Eugene V. Debs died in Lindlahr Sanitarium in Elmhurst only a few blocks from the Sandburg house. His death was another falling away of the past. Even though he had left the Socialist party almost a decade before, Carl had remained a good friend of Debs. Over the past five years he had faithfully visited the invalided crusader at the sanitarium. Much that socialism had stood for Sandburg still found good; indeed, he was beginning to see Socialistic principles legislated into law.

For several years he had been making platform appearances, always ending his programs with a group of folk songs sung to the accompaniment of his strumming guitar. He had collected such songs wherever he could in his travels, and he had solicited the aid of his friends in bringing together as many as possible. As a result he possessed nearly three hundred songs, many of which had never been in print. In 1927 Harcourt, Brace published *The American Songbag*, containing not only the words and music but an account of their history and sometimes the incidents surrounding the compiler's discovery.

Attracted by the success of *The Prairie Years*, the Hearst Syndicate offered Sandburg thirty thousand dollars a year to write a column, but he refused. His own vision might have its limitations in the sight of his critics, but he could not conform to what he felt was the myopia of the Hearst philosophy.

Besides, he was busy enough without this added responsibility.

In fact, he was in the way of becoming a celebrity. In June of 1928 he was honored as Phi Beta Kappa poet at Harvard. In return for his Phi Beta Kappa key he read his new poem, "Good Morning, America." He warned his listeners, appropriately enough, that truth cannot be equated with facts, for "Facts are phantom. . ." (*CP*, 321). In October this poem provided the title for his next book, *Good Morning, America,* which he dedicated to his friend and publisher Alfred Harcourt ("A. H.").

He had been pondering for several years the meaning of poetry, and accordingly prefaced this book with thirty-eight attempts at pinning it down—"Tentative (First-Model) Definitions of Poetry" (*CP*, 317–19). In these definitions Sandburg used imagery of all sorts to explain this paradoxical entwining of available material and the ultimately inexpressible. The best known of these thrusts into the dark called poetry a combination of "hyacinths and biscuits," dreams and flowers, yes, but practicalities and words, too. Language is frightening and awesome in its flexibility, connotations, and emotional impact, but it is the material substance ("biscuits") which a poet must use to try to communicate the ineffable ("hyacinths"). Through the use of imagery—the concrete—the poet tries to convey meaning beyond ("hyacinths") what the words can say literally ("biscuits").

On the "biscuits" side—the necessary means at the poet's disposal—Sandburg employed terminology ranging from the patency of "dots and dashes, spelling depths," "a search for syllables," "a type-font design," "silence and speech," "a statement of a series of equations," "static syllables" to "an enumeration of birds, bees, babies, butterflies, bugs, bambinos, babayagas, and bipeds," "the establishment of a metaphorical link," "a deliberate prism of words," "fire, smoke-stacks, waffles, pansies, people, and purple sunsets." Even in this list on the material side, metaphor is inevitable.

To indicate the indescribable effect—the "hyacinths"—Sandburg's vocabulary of definition ranged from "echoes," "the sixth sense and the fourth dimension," to "invisible keepsakes," "the sign of infinity." It is often in contrasts, however—in juxtaposition of the two sides to poetry (finite materials of words and images on the one hand and intention and effect beyond explanation on the other)—that Sandburg tried to come to grips with the problem of definition: "a shuffling of boxes of illusions buckled with a strap of facts," "the harnessing of the paradox of earth cradling life and then entombing it."

The poet, then, used two kinds of words in trying to get at the essence of his craft. The first set was composed of such objective, almost scientific, noncommittal words as "projection," "report," "plan," "theorem," "search," "series," "arrangement," "enumeration." The second kind was sensuous: "mirror," "balloon," "fossil rock-print," "shadow-dancer," "torn-up love-letters." Granted, the poem must appear on the page in some sort of order and it has to use words in two ways—literally and figuratively. Its purpose, however, is not mere reporting, but an evocation of emotion, a depth of meaning that a mere perusal of what meets the eye cannot produce. Sandburg made, therefore, a point of the arrangement. A poem must appear in a certain way upon a page, for this design contributes to the totality of its effect.

The pattern on the page must be new and even startling to bring the reader refreshment and insight as well as connotations beyond the literal meaning of the words themselves. The words are a breaking of the silence that surrounds us, not with the sole purpose of making an overt statement, but of hinting at that which in the long run is far off in the fogs of the inexpressible. Again and again Sandburg returned to the idea of meaning beyond hope of explication. This suggestion, this hinting, is to be achieved in part by paradox, by contrast. Poetry is an effort to give permanence to that which is, after all, only fleeting. The opportunity comes only momentarily and by chance, even to a man of keen intuition, of glimpsing the nuances that make all the difference between a pedestrian experience and a highly imaginative one. A poet's purpose is to capture these fragile and evanescent seconds in the comparative permanence of language. When he has done this, he will hope to have re-created the wonder and awe of the enveloping dark and silent night. Through its attempts to do the impossible, poetry itself becomes a metaphor for all man's aspirations, hopes, and desires.

In his definitions, Sandburg said little about the use of concrete images as things in themselves. Rather, he put emphasis first on the words and then on the transcending meaning that the words might evoke. The image, the sense impression described, would be only a way station toward a final intention, which would always be above logical clarification.

Sandburg may not be one of America's "difficult" poets, but in 1928 when he was writing verse, he plainly did not expect to be taken as a newspaper reporter, a historian, or even a biographer. But even in his biography of Lincoln, while being true to fact as he saw it, he practiced the art of arrangement of materials with a view to combining what he felt was clear, affective, and significant. To convey the affective, furthermore, a writer needs to choose words with appropriate connotations and even to employ the poetic device of metaphor in order to suggest the meaning beyond meaning that is the richest depth of poetry.

The ordering of the materials and the selection of language were important parts of the writer's craft. For Sandburg a third technique was the piling up of evidence. That he felt a compulsion to make thirty-eight "tentative" attempts at defining poetry shows how hard it is to focus on a simple explanation; but all thirty-eight taken together begin to give the impression of a meaning. In like manner he used the method of including everything available—fact, legend, commentary—in writing the biography of Lincoln, in the story of his own first twenty years (*Always the Young Strangers*), and in his novel, *Remembrance Rock* (1948). He did not intend these volumes to be a set of reference books for the reader to browse in and select details from (as Edmund Wilson has said the Lincoln books are). The author had actually already selected his materials. His intention was not division or subtraction, but multiplication and addition. By dint of sheer mass of matter, the effect of these prose works has been for some readers impressively (though for others *oppressively*) monumental. If, as historians have said, Sandburg's life of Lincoln is not really history, then probably the best parts are evocation—literature of the imagination—rather than factual statement and logical analysis. The same can be said for *Always the Young Strangers:* the events it describes are in themselves flat; the value of the book lies in its language and mood.

In the Preface to *Storm over the Land* (1942; taken largely from *The War Years,* 1939), he was to state his purpose in writing such prose. The reader can think that Sandburg would hope the same for all his work: that he was not writing a mere timekiller, not providing mere entertainment. He wanted his readers to find stimulating companions from the past (vivid characterization) as well as some instruction (apparently more from thoughtful reading and application than from didactic writing). One wonders, however, if the compilations that were to find culmination in *The People, Yes* (1936) were intended as didactic. They represent what wisdom the folk have. How much the people and the reader profit by repeating these hackneyed truisms is open to debate—or, at the very least, is virtually impossible to calculate.

Good Morning, America, a book of verse, met with a pleasant welcome.[6] Leon Whipple in *The Survey* was almost as rhapsodic as the poet himself. Taking his cue chiefly from the title poem, he described the book as "a paean to this gorgeous shield of American earth, its trees and waters, winds and stars, crickets and autumn leaves, melodious scents and endearing sounds." Horace Gregory compared Sandburg's relation to his country to Robert Burns's with Scotland: they both had taken poetry out of the complexly formal category and had distilled for it the speech of the inarticulate masses. Sandburg's "dry humor" impressed Babette Deutsch; for this quality, as well as his pervading awareness of the passing of time, made him different from his much-touted predecessor, Whitman. Though his satire was indeed mocking, it was not devastating, but gentle, warmed by his sense of humor. Mark Van Doren went so far as to say that Sandburg "knows better than any of his contemporaries how to put a flowing world on paper."

On the other side of the argument, however, Edwin Seaver in *The New Republic* found this new book weaker than earlier ones. Sandburg was, moreover, still incapable of establishing values and of articulating definite criticism of his America. As usual, his ideas disappeared in a haze whenever he tried to tell what life is all about. Whereas Gregory said that in this book Sandburg was showing evidence of a steady firming up of point of view, Seaver could see no progress at all. To him, Sandburg was exactly what he had been in 1914; he had nothing new to say and, what was worse, he was saying it with less vigor.

Another unhappy reviewer was Percy Hutchinson in the New York *Times Book Review*. Again, where Gregory admired Sandburg's use of the Midwest as a symbol for all America, Hutchinson opined that Sandburg's parochialism was keeping him from being successful. Furthermore, Hutchinson objected to the technique of accumulation, the cataloguing which reminded many readers of Whitman; and he was irritated by the formlessness (another seeming link with Whitman), which he equated with a deliberate lack of discipline. That Sandburg longed for beauty was not to be questioned, but, despite nuances in pace and variation in mood, the paucity of engaging intricacy and subtlety was disturbing.

These remarks of the reviewers—all of them responsible, all experienced, all wide readers—boil down to the inescapable fact that criticism is, in the end, mostly a matter of current fashion and personal taste. Some readers, and discriminating ones at that, find Sandburg satisfying; others (Edmund Wilson among them) find him almost totally unappealing. And it is not possible to say that the answer must lie somewhere in between. For it is obvious that the answer is to be found in the fact that for thirty-five years the vogue has been the complications of Pound and Eliot rather than the simplicities and candid puzzlements, quite unresolved, of Carl Sandburg.

Though he may not have a blueprint for the future, he does show strength in his expression of the minutiae of life. He is a poet to be read not *in toto* nor even in great slabs, but at short sittings. He is what might be called a "spare-minute" poet, for his intimate glimpses, his brief expressions of mood, idea, longing, his landscapes and personal etchings, are pleasing—even stimulating—for a limited reading. His talkiness and his tendency to all inclusiveness make the search for the penetrating line, the memorable observation, and the occasional fresh combination of images sometimes, quite frankly, a tiring one. What Sandburg needs more than anything else is a sympathetic but severe editor.

Good Morning, America is divided into nine sections, the first being the title poem. The others have characteristic labels: "Corn Belt," "Valley Mist," "Little Album," "Bitter Summer Thoughts," "Rain Winds," "Great Rooms," "Sky Pieces," and "Timber Moon." With the exception of "Corn Belt" (which pictures the Midwest with nostalgia under such titles as "Corn Prattlings" and "Haze Gold") and of "Bitter Summer Thoughts" (which contains a few expressions of loneliness, misunderstanding, and unfulfilled ambition) these section headings have little significance. "Valley Mist," for example, presents views not only of the prairie, but also of Cincinnati, New York, Ashtabula, Chillicothe (ambiguously identifying the place with Illinois, Missouri, and Ohio, all of which have a town by that name), and of Santa Fe, in a ten-part poem called "Santa Fe Sketches" (*CP*, 373–78).

The general theme of this last poem is the patience of that old city, its capacity for taking events as they come. This motif Sandburg had exploited frequently before, notably in "Prairie." He was quite thoroughly obsessed with the comparative permanence of such natural phenomena as the Great Plains and the Western deserts in contrast with the transience of human beings, though the flow of humanity, too, struck him as inexhaustible. (Robinson Jeffers saw nature as outlasting man, but his view of humanity was not so generous as Sandburg's.)

"She Opens the Barn Door Every Morning" at the beginning of "Corn Belt" (*CP*, 344) is a Whitmanesque genre piece in the form of an address to a farm "woman heavy with the earth,/ Clean as a milk pail washed in the sun. . . ." "Poplar and Elm," "Brown Gold," "Ripe Corn," "Cornfield Ridge and Stream" continue the picture technique. They are landscapes etched with love—sometimes peopled, sometimes not.

The juxtaposition of prosiness and of sudden lyric loveliness can be demonstrated in "Crossing Ohio When Poppies Bloom in Ashtabula," (*CP*, 365). The road-atlas clarity and flatness of "near the northwest corner of Pennsylvania" lacks intensity, insight, tenderness, strength—in short, it lacks everything and anything that would qualify it as a line of poetry. Even in context it is unsuccessful. Down the page in the same poem occurs a sentence almost mawkish in both content and arrangement on the page: "Pick me poppies in Ohio,/mother. . . ." The use of the word "mother" is distasteful here for two reasons: it is superficially emotional in its connotation, and it is given undue, affected emphasis by its placement on a separate line. Thus it destroys for the sensitive reader any feeling of rising poetic intensity. Yet it is followed by an imaginative description of a

back yard full of poppies: "seven sunsets saved themselves/to
be here now." These two clauses, both on the same page, demon-
strate that the complaint about Sandburg is legitimate enough:
one must search, often too hard, to find a line worth saving.
Sandburg's taste frequently failed him, despite his own protest
that he picked, polished, and perfected every line.

On the other hand, Seaver's comment that here Sandburg was
showing signs of decreasing vigor would need heavy qualifica-
tion. It was a good thing in the eyes of many that he was no
longer pounding his manly chest and shouting virile curses in
his joy at being alive. If Seaver missed such exhibition, many
others interpreted it as a tempering of former raucousness. They
were grateful for Sandburg's continuing interest in his America,
its prairies and cities. Sentimentality, it is true, was not lacking in
the book. "They Ask: Is God, Too, Lonely?" concludes that He
is. "Epistle," about the love of Jesus for his environment and
friends in Galilee, is banal and obvious. But other poems are
strong and none the less manly for being quieter.

Both Babette Deutsch and Horace Gregory considered
"Again?" a good poem (*CP*, 368). Thirty-three lines long, it
develops the favorite motif of "Why?". With the millions he
had accumulated from ten-cent sales, Woolworth had con-
structed a skyscraper and had left enough of a fortune for his
widow to build another if she wanted to. Query: What do skyscrapers mean? Sandburg never knows; he never even specu-
lates. He just poses the question. This characteristic is what
irritates his detractors. Those who take pleasure in reading him,
however, do not seem to be annoyed by his unresolved interro-
gations.

Again other poems which merit consideration, "Snatch of
Sliphorn Jazz" uses the dotted rhythms of jazz improvisation
supported by the familiar slang of "kid," "doggone," and "bust."
Its theme is not new—finding happiness where one is, but modi-
fying it with the realization of the passing of time.

> But not happy-happy, kid, don't
> be too doubled-up doggone happy.
> (*CP*, 420)

"Precious Moments," like several other poems, concerns itself
with the responsibilities one bears for his vocabulary, his

means—and power—of communication. In *Slabs of the Sunburnt West*, "Primer Lesson" had emitted a sharp warning to be very careful about the use of words, for once uttered, they are virtually irrevocable. In "Precious Moments" man is admonished to heed his utterances, for

> In the moment of doom when the word forms
> It is born, alive, registering an imprint—
> Afterward it is a mummy, a dry fact, done and gone.
>
> (*CP*, 428)

Language is an awesome thing. It must be used with care.

It is the title poem, however, that is the most impressive in the book (*CP*, 320–26). In spite of the frequently expressed opinion that Sandburg's best is to be found only in his briefer impressions, "Good Morning, America" maintains on the whole continuity both in development of idea and in intensity of expression. Next to the book-length *The People, Yes* (1936), it is Sandburg's longest and most ambitious piece of poetry. Composed of twenty-one sections, it is basically, as Whipple said, "a paean to this great gorgeous shield of American earth": but it moves through a variety of moods and does not sustain a peak of ecstasy to the point of weariness.

As evening comes on, the poet is moved to ask who built the cities, and, of course, the answer is "the little two-legged joker, Man." He is aware of the absurdity of man's condition, thrown as he is into this cage and given what amounts to a curse of freedom: the necessity of making decisions that will bring him to at least mortal fulfillment (the agnostic view). So, though man is a "joker," he is a builder too.

Then Sandburg devotes several sections to a discussion of the "facts." Mountains and waterfalls are undeniably part of the landscape: they are facts, apparently permanent, but in the long run fleeting (in the history of the cosmos). A tiny bluebird examines Niagara Falls and wonders what this is all about. (The gray mouse in "Slabs of the Sunburnt West" had been as much a part of nature as the walls of the Grand Canyon.)

All facts have the paradoxical quality of being both lasting and ephemeral. Though God is a fact for many, a man will interpret God according to his temperament and circumstance. No final understanding of the fact of God will be possible until greater flights—by implication flights of the spirit—take place than those of current nature (butterflies) and of current mankind (airplanes). But a man's particular faith in his kind of God is, for him, nevertheless a fact.

Facts include statues of heroes (representatives of history), flowers of every classification (catalogues—*à la* Whitman—of flowers native to several states), and seeds and eggs. If man could get at the secret of the egg, he would have the answer to the eternal question—man's source and purpose.

America had a beginning (a metaphorical egg), but its past holds no key to the problem. Though reviewing her history briefly, the poet maintains the view he held in "Prairie" that "the past is a bucket of ashes." So he turns his attention to the facts of the present activity in American civilization and to the description of that activity through mass communication and the people's slogans, of which he supplies a fairly lengthy list, ending with "Keep your shirt on." (He had made similar collections in *The Prairie Years* and was to carry the practice to handbook proportions in *The People, Yes.*) These are the people's means of expressing what they experience and know in terms of the familiar, comfortable, and generally undisturbing proverb. These proverbs may be unchallenging, but they are suitable to what Sandburg knows of the unthinking populace, whom he loves in spite of its stupidity, whom he admires for its lack of pretense, for its rough good humor, and above all for its patience.

Next he turns his attention to the ever-present imminence of death. On the general level, Sandburg shows that pioneers and profiteers alike return to dust; graft and corruption do not stave off death. Even whole civilizations pass into obscurity. The United States is now on top of the heap, giving at least lip-service to God, but actually worshiping efficiency and speed. Individually, Death the Sleepwalker haunts us and makes us ponder; but, if we are sensible, we are willing to accept it as inevitable and not to worry about it. We are too busy with the richness of everyday living to be afraid; so we give an optimistic morning greeting to everybody and to all our doubts and queries.

But our country bids fair to last a long time. Even though an understanding of our basic situation is still a long way off, life will go on. Sandburg suggests that we give ourselves up to the job of living—work, play, and meditation.

Sea sunsets, give us keepsakes.
Prairie gloamings, pay us for prayers.
Mountain clouds on bronze skies—
    Give us great memories.
Let us have summer roses.
Let us have tawny harvest haze in pumpkin time.
Let us have springtime faces to toil for and play for,
Let us have the fun of booming winds on long waters.
Give us dreamy blue twilights—of winter evenings—to wrap us
    in a coat of dreaminess.
Moonlight, come down—shine down, moonlight—meet every bird
    cry and every song calling to a hard old earth, a sweet young
    earth.   (*CP*, 336)

In "Good Morning, America," Sandburg had woven a web of great variety of color, rhythm, mood, and time callused and ancient and yet fresh and lovely. Time may pass, evanescence may be a fact, but in America there is always the joy of renewal.

All of Sandburg is in this poem: his brashness, his tenderness, his humor, his clichés, his insights, his awe, his noisiness (despite Seaver's opinion), his quiet, his querying, and his acceptance. Some judgments to the contrary, a case can be made for "Good Morning, America" as a highly effective poem. Like almost any poem, it gains in emotional thrust if read aloud.

CHAPTER 6

The People and the Union

I *The Move to Michigan*

DURING THE NEXT SEVERAL YEARS Sandburg produced a variety of books. It is this varied talent that makes him hard to categorize. About the time of the publication of *Good Morning, America* he pondered the possibilities of writing a novel concerning the whole of America, the sweep of her greatness. He had even thought of a title—*From Coast to Coast*. Other matters, however, were pressing for his attention. So he set aside the idea—for the time being.

In January, 1929, *Steichen the Photographer* lauded briefly the poet's brother-in-law and his work. The essay served as a biographical introduction to a collection of Steichen's photographs, some of them taken from advertisements. In detailing some of the events of the subject's life, the final effect of the book was like patchwork. Sandburg obviously was fond of Steichen, and he had a natural enthusiasm for photography. So there was a certain vitality in the telling, but the language was chiefly colloquial and inclined to be blatant: he wrote of "a certain loud-mouthed busybody and faker of the art world" (64); he said in the opening that "Mr. Morgan was willing. It was okeh with him" (5). Interesting though the anecdotes might be, one must conclude that the diction was often entirely unsuited to the purpose of preparing the reader for the elegant, though now dated, photographs which followed. At any rate, it was an introductory essay and need not be of further concern as a piece of literature.

In the spring of 1930 appeared *Potato Face*, more Rootabaga stories. Though the author hoped they would have adult appeal, their chief readers proved to be children. Toward the end of this year he published a selection of his verses that would be interesting to children. He called the book *Early Moon* (after one of the poems), and he prefaced it with a sixteen-page "Short Talk on Poetry." As in his thirty-eight definitions, he reached no totally satisfactory conclusions in these ruminations. He said that a poet uses words; beyond that, the ingredients are for all intents and purposes indescribable.

His great interest in the life of Lincoln brought him to a consideration of Mrs. Lincoln, who was the subject of a narrative-essay in 1932, *Mary Lincoln, Wife and Widow.* It defended the thesis that Mary Todd had suffered since childhood from a cerebral disease and therefore could not be entirely responsible for her often high-handed acts, which Lincoln had to bear with increasing patience and eventually with pity. Sandburg followed her through her life, from childhood through courtship and the twenty-two years of married life to the years after her husband's assassination, when she suffered national condemnation for much of what Lincoln had sustained. Sandburg's efforts at fairness and objectivity were marred by his own inability to see beyond his love for Lincoln and by his partisan identification with his hero. His style was the cozy, informal, colloquial one he had used in the *Steichen,* and it was as out of place in working on a psychiatric thesis as it had been in introducing the elegant photographs of his brother-in-law. What may have contributed to an air of spontaneity in *The Prairie Years* here seemed somewhat awkward and self-conscious. The second section of the book—the larger part—was correspondence and other documents (edited by Paul M. Angle) from which Sandburg had developed his theme.

In this same year of 1932 he left the Chicago *Daily News* and moved his family permanently to Harbert. The house, under Paula's expert direction, was reconstructed to make it right for year-round living. The family had become interested in raising goats. So Paula, too, supervised the building of suitable quarters for their growing herd. They named the place "Chicaming Goat Farm."

From now on, Sandburg settled down seriously to the development of materials concerning Lincoln's last four years. He had planned some day to write three or four chapters on Lincoln's life in the White House. At first he thought he might add them as a kind of epilogue to *The Prairie Years;* then he considered them as a possible prologue—presenting a sketch of the obligations and honors of being Chief Executive—to a book that would tell the American story of humble origins and the rise to eminence. He now found, however, that the documents were too massive for such summary treatment. He decided to undertake a detailed continuation of the two-volume work he had completed. The job would take a long time, but he had a brilliant and helpful wife and also three daughters—Janet, Margaret, and Helga—who would find the task an adventure.

His newspaper responsibilities behind him, he changed his routines. With less feeling of compulsion, he slowed down somewhat, began working at night and sleeping late into the morning. He found gaps in the story that needed filling. He spent his hours organizing and planning. In addition to his family, now and then a secretary was called in to assist. During the warm months, April to October, he labored away at the Lincoln biography; but he also found time to write letters, to sing folk songs, to undertake essays, and to compose poetry. Then during the winter months he traveled, making public appearances reading his poems and singing his songs. In 1934 he went as far as the University of Hawaii to deliver a series of lectures. Wherever he went, he assiduously hunted down what information relevant to his big project was available.

II *The People, Yes*

One of the products of the ingathering of Lincolniana was an accumulation of the aphorisms of the people. From the sheafs of notes Sandburg had taken through the years, he collected the materials that could be listed as folk wisdom and strung them together loosely on a thread of affirmation, of assurance that the masses would someday get their due. The resulting book, *The People, Yes,* was published in 1936. Since the Great Depression was still a reality, the new volume had a special timeliness: the people needed encouragement. This book (*CP*, 439–617) purported to be the voice of the long-suffering common man, alternating with the vatic promises of the poet himself. A combination of catalogue and commentary, it was at first glance a kind

of catch-all of folklore and rhapsodic flights. For sheer massive-
ness of detail the book was impressive. Divided into 107 sections, it consisted of proverbs, anecdotes, yarns, clichés, biographies, legends, character sketches, folk-wisdom, dialogues—all
against a background of observations and prophecies in Sandburg's own idiom, sometimes mystical, sometimes slangy.

If most of *The People, Yes* would not qualify as poetry,
enough original and imaginative lines connected the tried and
true sayings to make the reader at least ponder on the problem
of classification of the work. Americana it undoubtedly was,
both prose and *vers libre* in identifiable Sandburg rhythms, for
now and then the poet had attained some degree of intensity,
which is the most distinguishing mark of true poetry, but for
the most part he had simply made an enchiridion of folk-litera-
ture. *The People, Yes* is on the whole of more potential interest
to the sociologist and the historian—or to a newcomer to America—than to a student of imaginative literature. Occasional
change of pace, of mood, and of diction does not alter the fact
that only a small portion of the book can qualify as poetry. The
rest is a catalogue of information, no doubt very useful for the
reading and writing of literature, but not actually literature
itself.

The People, Yes was a full-length development of a concept
Sandburg had long entertained. Sometime before he moved to
Chicago to work on the short-lived Chicago *World,* he had
written a brief poem which he titled "I Am the People, the
Mob." He had included it in the final section of *Chicago Poems,*
called "Other Days (1900–1910)." Its eight lines of varying
length stated the thesis on which he was to base most of his
socialist-influenced poems: the people do the chores of the
world; the people sometimes rise in revolt, but soon quiet down
again. Their difficulty comes from their facility in forgetting
their grievances and in letting themselves be cheated all over
again. Their salvation can come only when they learn to use the
misery of the past to spur them on to action for a better future:
"The mob—the crowd—the mass—will arrive then" (*CP,* 71).
Such a spirit had been pervading the whole of Sandburg's verse
for more than thirty years. The purpose of *The People, Yes* was
to explore fully the concepts of that early eight-line statement.

Only in the broadest, and most liberal, sense does a coherent

line of reasoning etch its way through the book. (The early brief
poem had moved logically from fact to analysis to promise.) A
rapid survey of the pages shows much repetition and back-track-
ing. An argument of a sort, however, is discernible.

In its opening pages (Sections 1–5) *The People, Yes* asserts
that, though the Tower of Babel was an unsuccessful experiment, the common people the world over still ask the same
questions (in spite of the differences in the symbols of their
languages): they still want to know, as did the builders of the
ill-fated Tower, their identity, their next move, and their ultimate destiny. These three problems are a kind of refrain, a link-
ing device for the various parts of the book. The questions arise
in Illinois and Indiana. The answer is always silence, the silence
which explains, though it does not defend, why Sandburg had
made the same inquiries throughout the years without offering
the slightest inkling of a concrete plan of salvation beyond
"Wake up!" Unfortunately, he lost many readers for just this
very reason—that he had been unable to take the risk of even
a tentative solution or suggestion for the world's ills. He got lost
in a fog before he could see even the faint outlines of a rock
of rescue. In the book he goes on to say that people are condi-
tioned by the land they spring from, whether it be Texas, the
desert, Cleveland, Greece, the Mississippi, Kentucky, or Knox
County, Illinois. But no matter what their language, no matter
what their customs, no matter what their reactions to individual
circumstances, the three big questions remain the same: Who
am I? What do I do next? What is my ultimate purpose?

Dreams are more powerful than death, for it is dreams that
make the world go round (Sections 6–8). (He had said the same
thing in 1906 in his foreword to Wright's *The Dreamer*.) Seeking
to kill those who have wronged one is not worth the effort, for
the effects of revenge do not last. Dreams are another matter:
they endure beyond mere death. For example Eastman—the
Kodak man—having dreamed, through his last will and testament, of all the good his money could do, committed suicide
before he could change the provisions. He was determined that
his dreams should outlast the moment of his death. But a man
must do more than merely dream (Section 9–10). He must learn
to profit by every experience, no matter how insignificant or how
saddening. (How like the seventeenth-century Massachusetts

Puritans this sounds!) Especially is the experience of solitude important to the understanding of self, to the establishment of identity. In a way, too, solitude permits one to dream, to hope, to plan, and so to contribute to man's destiny. But important though dreaming is, one should learn to be moderate in expectations. (At fifty-eight, Sandburg had lost some of the energetic fervor of his Wisconsin days.) Human nature being what it is, a man's aspirations should always exceed his achievement; otherwise, he will wither in complacency.

After recounting some Russian legends, Sandburg says these are now lost in "thin smoke" (Sections 11–19). Then he says that the people too "move/in a fine thin smoke. . ." (*CP*, 451). This transition to one of his favorite topics is not very clear, unless he means that the people, like the legends of Russia, come from a past that is hazy and possibly pointless. Sandburg's view of history and the past is somewhat ambiguous. From one side of his mouth he says that history is useless ("a bucket of ashes"); from the other side, that only when the people learn to remember, to profit from the past, will they come into their own. At any rate, Sandburg sees the people now as the arch on which the structure of civilization depends. They may live by instinct, but they still ask the basic questions. And with all their asking, they do the work of the world. They form the armies and die for their countries; then after the war they build the peace, for they thrive on hope. The common people may be for some scholars and leaders an abstract idea, a generality, a sociological concept; but they are here to stay. It is their small-change purchases, for example, that make the economy and incidentally create economic despots. An abstraction or not, the plain folk too have their unheralded heroes who give to the utmost in the game of life (which at best is a gamble).

Now Sandburg turns his attention to a problem (Sections 20–26) that had beset him from the beginning of his career: who can be adequate spokesman for the people? They are so vast that no one can know all that they do or think, but they are indispensable and should have a record. They have knowledge of considerable importance right now, and they learn more as the years roll on—about death, about sorrow, about getting through life. They need a poet, a man who is both "earthworm" and "rider to the moon," one who can express their daily deeds and their great aspirations; for they have learned the values of living one day at a time, yet they will outlast history—if history means great men and mighty acts (and Sandburg is back to the sociological mass!).

History records the tortures and the bravery of the people as they have relied on faith (Sections 27–31). In American history, as in all history, the people, whether "a great beast" or not, have done the work of creating the new country. The poet reiterates a frequent thesis—that leaders and governments pass, but the people continue, drawing on their experience for a slow accretion of wisdom. "Time is a great teacher." How do "the people learn"? Through painful experience—through work, through disappointment, through deception (Sections 32–68). They can learn the immediate: That is, though they may be stupid, they can follow directions for now. The trouble is, they are too easily duped. Sandburg uses the chameleon as subject of a vague metaphor for the changeable demagogue, the unreliable, the liar. Even Napoleon lied to himself, told himself he was greater than he really was: if a common man can see through such boastful deception in the world's heroes, he is ready to know himself. In a brief, eloquent passage Sandburg says that the message of the restless wind and sea is that man will always be going somewhere, but that he will never actually attain his goal (any more than did Napoleon):

> The sea moves always, the wind moves always.
> They want and want and there is no end to their wanting.
> What they sing is the song of the people.
> Man will never arrive, man will be always on the way.
> It is written he shall rest but never for long.
> The sea and the wind tell him he shall be lonely, meet love, be
> shaken with struggle, and go on wanting.
>
> (CP, 479)

But even so, he will always focus on the now, the present, one day at a time. For it is from the present that he learns. Basically, men are all alike, but money creates differences, and the rights of property on the one hand and the right to work on the other create problems. The fact remains, however, that kings and beggars have precisely the same experience—birth, trouble, death. Their problems may crystallize into superstitions, into apothegms and stock jokes, but all ends in death. Poverty, basic naïveté, a natural tendency to be stubborn—all contribute, if perversely, to the knowledge of the people. Such an everyday commodity as eggs enters the folklore and the vernacular. It takes an Agassiz (and a Sandburg?) to see the entire universe in a single egg. The people are not so subtly philosophic as that. Their knowledge is couched more boldly, more immediately, more availably, in yarns, anecdotes, and legends (Rip Van Winkle, Mike Fink, Paul Bunyan).

Sandburg devotes all of Section 57 (*CP*, 521-25) to an analysis of Lincoln chiefly by quotation. He follows the questionable device of spacing some of Lincoln's utterances in free verse, partly to fit the pattern of the rest of the book, partly to prove that Lincoln had the mind of a poet. It is clear that he feels Lincoln worthy of a pedestal.

The people as a force go about their daily chores, meet their troubles, endure their miseries with a sense of humor. Common sense pulls them through the most rugged experiences. They cannot expect much relief, however, as long as money is the greatest source of power. Rich and poor alike must die, but meanwhile there are those problems—in economics and in politics, both of which have a great deal to do with the problems of unemployment in an increasingly technical age. Newspapermen (Sandburg was writing from experience) are especially in a position to see the underhandedness and duplicity, in the face of which they cultivate a protective cynicism.

Even in the matter of law and justice, money talks, though a lawyer, like any other professional man, will have his tales of defense (Sections 69–85). (At this point, Sandburg begins a motif of threat: the people is a mob till organized: "The mob is a beginning, man lacking concert" [*CP*, 553]. Even omnipotent dictators depend on the ever-flowing mass of humanity. This motif plays a more and more ominous role as the book proceeds.) A judge is only a man; a jury is only "twelve names out of a hat"; oaths are useless, for no one can possibly know "the whole truth" (just as, though the sun and the moon are known to everyone, they are different phenomena to different people). So the poor, the laboring classes, will always get a raw deal; but Sandburg has hope that equity will be the eventual victor. He has a vision that time is sure to be on the side of the people. "The flowing of the stream clears it of pollution" (*CP*, 562).

The sea is a symbol of the power of the people to absorb all things, hence even to overcome injustice.

> The bottom of the sea accommodates mountain ranges.
> This is how deep the sea is
> And the toss and drip of the mystery of the people
> And the sting of sea-drip.
> In the long catacombs of moss fish linger and move
> Hearing the cries of the dolphins while they too wander.
> This is the depot of lost and unreclaimed baggage, . . .
> (*CP*, 562-63)

But such a destiny is now still hidden in the far-distant future; all is mist, haze, reverie. Meanwhile, the folk attend to the daily tasks—making paper sacks, making so many mittens that the maker sees mittens in everything, including the shape of evergreens. But time passes and man's hopes and accomplishments come to dust, in spite of the temporal assurance that money would appear to give.

The poet is now concerned again about his inadequacy for expressing his subject: "Who can make a poem of the depths of weariness. . . ?" (*CP*, 570). The target of all crafty men is the people, who nevertheless go on and on in spite of death, constantly looking for just the next step. Where is the poet who can express them?

As the poem approaches its close, the threat motif reappears (Sections 86–101): "The people have the element of surprise./ Where are the kings today?" (*CP*, 576). Sane, balanced, disciplined men are rare, but some day there will be many of them. Today the laboring people do and make everything, stumblingly moving forward. They may be slow, but they are inexorable. No justice can be found in the way people are currently pushed around. Hiring and firing, cheating and duping go on day after day. Few in high places care about the welfare of the poor.

Here once more Sandburg confesses that even after years of concern and of trying to be the spokesman of the underprivileged, he must admit defeat.

The unemployed
.   .   .   .

these lead to no easy pleasant conversation
they fall into a dusty disordered poetry.
(CP, 607)

Through the years Sandburg had not known how successful he was, whether he was actually writing poetry or not, whether he was presenting his case with necessary clarity and intensity. He here admits that his subject has been of such nature as to preclude a bright and ordered verse—a kind of self-defense against most of his adverse critics.

In the last sections of the book (Sections 102–7) the poet makes a vague prophecy that the people will eventually win out. Leaders simply cannot debauch the minds of the masses and expect to keep the peace. Revolution will come; tomorrow will bring an inevitable change. History (that ambiguous entity) has frequently produced first murmurs, then revolt. Sandburg hears the people murmuring now. Propaganda comes and goes in waves, but the people outlast it and its effects, even though they may temporarily succumb. He bids the people to rouse from their slumbers.

The last section, a coda of sorts, returns to the first statement: the people plod onward, do all the work, cherish their hopes, griefs, and aspirations.

> In the darkness with a great bundle of grief the
> people march,
> In the night, and overhead a shovel of stars for
> keeps, the people march:
> > "Where to? what next?"
> > (CP, 617)

Thus runs the "argument" of the poem. It is repetitious beyond a doubt—as even this summation had to be. In objective statement it says nothing which Sandburg had not said a hundred times before. Except for rare passages it is devoid of heightened effect, but stays on the level of prose most of the way. Its chief virtue is that of a compendium, a catalogue, a sourcebook. It would do well to have an index.

Sandburg now was a Roosevelt Democrat in sympathy if not in declaration. *The People, Yes,* which he gave to his country when the Great Depression had drained the country of hope, of enterprise, of energy, had about it an aura of Rooseveltian optimism, however vaguely defined the goals. The people might be ignorant and gullible, but they had many admirable qualities, as he had said many times before—a sense of humor, shrewdness, toughness, and dignity. For some readers the book was unsatisfactory because of the persisting propaganda without program and because of the sociological focus on the mass, the crowd. Other readers were not unhappy with these typically Sandburg characteristics. They simply accepted them and went on to other considerations.

Though for the most part the book was a thesaurus, an enchiridion, even the passages recording the clichés of the people were useful. The outline of the book was not very clear, but it showed a semblance of development, a skeleton of organization. The flesh of the book was the catalogues, the tales, the little life histories, the earthy and hard-bitten proverbs, the jokes. Taken piecemeal, they appeared to be shaken up and thrown out in a jumble. But careful reading shows that they were supporting a fairly definite outline, ending in an attempt at communicating the qualities of hope and indestructibility in the book's hero—the people.

Sandburg had been the first poet of modern times actually to use the language of the people as his almost total means of expression. In 1798 Wordsworth had approached the problem, but he had not really put the common idiom down on paper. Sandburg had entered into the language of the people; he was not looking at it as a scientific phenomenon or a curiosity (as had H. L. Mencken). He was at home with it.

> The mazuma, the jack, the shekels, the kale,
> The velvet, the you-know-what,
> The what-it-takes, a roll, a wad,
> Bring it home, boy.
> Bring home the bacon.
>
> (*CP*, 541)

This book was the culmination of his career as poet. In earlier books he had made limited use of the Whitmanesque catalogue technique which he here had exploited. Morton Dauwen Zabel, in the most penetrating review[1] of *The People, Yes,* said that each of Sandburg's books had canceled out its predecessors because the poet had never changed his views nor his technique. This criticism one must deny in part: *Chicago Poems* had been raucous in spots and tender in others; *Cornhuskers* had turned to the prairies with awe and a more universally gentle voice; if *Smoke and Steel* had returned to the city, it had nevertheless added to the store of Sandburg portraits, to the landscape and street views, and it was less angry than *Chicago Poems,* more devoted to pity; the two long poems in *Slabs of the Sunburnt West* had great variety of mood and image; *Good Morning, America* had demonstrated a yet greater wisdom and less blasting out at the evils of capitalism. To ignore these books and read only *The People, Yes* would be to lose a good deal of the Sandburg flavor. If a reader had the patience and interest, he would be able to find in all six volumes many memorable pictures and many imaginative lines. But one would have to search and select.

Zabel speculated that, if Sandburg had had a definitely articulated creed (one cannot doubt but that his heart was right) and if he had been willing to work in the direction of more formal structure, his poetry would have been firmer and more profound. One is inclined to agree and to add that, if he had put as much energy into the shaping of lines as he had into word choice, the effect would have been more penetrating and nearer the ideal of good poetry. But he had not. What he had produced in this last book was a loosely jointed outline filled in with much plain prosaic statement, some hollow flights of fancy, and a few passages of quite exalted lyricism.

III   *The War Years*

The People, Yes out of his system, Sandburg turned his full attention to Lincoln's years in the White House. As the end of the work approached, he drove himself hard, rarely leaving his house on the dunes. By August, 1938, the manuscript had grown to such proportions that he began to wonder if anyone would want to wade through it. A book of such length, too, presented special problems in organization and emphasis.

His friend Lloyd Lewis of the Chicago *Daily News* read the manuscript of the entire first draft and was tremendously excited. Only in a few places did he suggest modifications of any sort. The closing chapters, relating to the assassination and the national mourning, particularly moved him. There Sandburg had departed from his usual objective reporting and had written, so his friend thought, a kind of symphony both grand and tragic. With Lewis's comments to guide him and to spur him on, he worked very hard through the winter. While he was writing, revising, and rewriting the chapter on Lincoln's death, he felt as if he were giving up a dear and sympathetic friend. He had been Lincoln's companion for years. The relationship had come to mean so much to him that he shed tears.

Sandburg went to Brooklyn with the manuscript in the spring of 1939 and spent five months in the home of Isabel Ely Lord, with whose help he prepared the typescript ˆfor the printers, read proofs, indexed the pages, and captioned the pictures. At long last the task was done. On December 3, *Abraham Lincoln: The War Years* was reviewed prominently in the book-review sections of both the New York *Herald-Tribune* and the New York *Times*. Over the country the book received approbation. If there were negative criticisms, they were almost totally swallowed up in admiration at what Sandburg had created: nearly twenty-five hundred pages in four volumes, detailing as never before in a single work the years of the Civil War. The price was twenty dollars a set. The publication date had been just in time for the Christmas trade. In only a few months the publishers had sold twenty-nine thousand sets. Sandburg the American was reaping the full harvest of the American way.

Ten days after the publication, the *Times* published an interview[2] which tried to present to the readers as much as possible about Sandburg's method of composition. Said Sandburg:

Lloyd Lewis . . . said there were patches without enough color. I thought that over, but I wasn't doing a Beethoven job—it is nearer Sibelius. It is bleak. There is no entertainment in it. Blocks of fact.

. . . I had cut down the sketch of Jefferson Davis to fifteen hundred words. [John] Hervey thought that wasn't enough. Lincoln's arch-antagonist given a page or so; bad proportion. So I built that up. I did a lot of tearing down and building.

Of the chapter on Lincoln's jokes and anecdotes, he said: "I sliced and chopped and rewrote and, even when it was down to its present size, I wasn't sure it would fit, if there would be a place for it. But finally the place was there and it fitted in." He had been a conscientious craftsman. In spite of the end result of a piling of fact on fact, he had tried for definite effects and emphases; and, according to most reviewers, he had succeeded in building an honest monument to a monumental hero.

Of the central figure of Lincoln, the author said that

> . . . his two salient characteristics were his sadness and his humor—a sadness born of sympathy and understanding, and a humor which ran from the finest threads of irony to the coarseness of the livery stable.
>
> He came from a breed and a region where the language of Shakespeare still persisted, and he knew the value of obsolete words and did not hesitate to use them. He developed a style which was the result of natural feeling, deep thought, and his early environment. He had a poet's sense of rhythm.

Sandburg might well have said much the same thing about himself. That his style was "developed" there is no doubt, for he often spent months in research and revision. That this style had grown out of his own basic emotions all critics were agreed upon. If by "deep thought" he meant profound concern, a weighing of values, and an ultimate indestructible stand, Sandburg could likewise have been describing himself. Furthermore, his language and the arrangement of the words were simple, unsophisticated, candid—the product of his Midwest. Finally, at his best, Sandburg, even in his prose works, "had a poet's sense of rhythm." Sandburg saw this himself. After he had received world acclaim for his life of Lincoln, he said, "I think that there is little in my biographical work when it approaches my best that I could not space into free verse." [3]

Five months after the publication of *The War Years* its author received the Pulitzer Prize in the category of history rather than biography. After all, though he had made Lincoln the center of his work, he had given his readers a thickly detailed accounting of the crucial four years that had settled once and for all the American principle of the union of the States.

In *The War Years* he had the materials for reaching his full height as storyteller, poet, and artist. Whereas the sources for *The Prairie Years* had been by comparison meager, now he had had literally thousands of books and letters and government documents to make use of. Because *The Prairie Years* had drawn from fewer sure accounts, it had relied on more guesses and had (this was probably the reason) been more lyrical (and sometimes more indistinct) as Sandburg strove to communicate the spirit of the life and times of the prairie Lincoln on the basis of a great deal of legend, tale, and hearsay. In fact, *The Prairie Years* might well now be considered as a poetic prologue to the four-volume account of Lincoln in Washington, an interesting reversal of the author's original intent.

The War Years itself was more of a conventionally historical work than its predecessor. Lacking footnotes (an omission irritating to the scholarly), with only occasional offhand references in the text itself, these volumes contained, nevertheless, hundreds of direct quotations from newspapers, letters, and other respectable documents that would give any history a distinct authenticity. The opening bibliographical essay was helpful as far as it went. It made incidental comment on the source materials and displayed flashes of pleasant humor. As a matter of fact, the author never ventured far from his evidence—rarely came to conclusions or expressed original insights; he trusted the material to speak for itself. Except for a few musical outbursts and introspective musings, generally speaking it was the facts piled one on the other in great heaps that gave the sympathetic reader the feeling of complexity and urgency characteristic of the four years of the Civil War as Lincoln had experienced them.

The Lincoln that Sandburg pictured was the Lincoln of the people. Wealthy, poverty-stricken, urban, rural, prominent, obscure, friendly, hostile—all had opinions about the President, and all were given their say in this book. If the author showed Lincoln slowly and patiently shaping the policies of his country, he also showed him paying generous and sympathetic attention to the least of citizens and quietly making those decisions that many executives would scorn. This concern with everyday, seemingly unimportant details, however, added up to statesmanship.

Through Sandburg's thorough account the reader sees how Lincoln made himself at last master of his position, how in spite of opportunity to set himself up as dictator he did not betray his country under the pretenses of the necessities of war. Sandburg shows that what seemed like Lincoln's aimlessness, his seeming inability to go directly to the heart of a matter, was in reality the work of genius, drawing nearer and nearer to his goal of restoration of the Union and of reconstruction on an equitable basis. (He points out that the emancipation of the slaves was forced on Lincoln by the piling up of events.)

In fact, Sandburg manages to communicate the point of view that Lincoln himself thought of his task as being beyond the power of a mere man to achieve. Paradoxically, the author shows him to have felt a tenderness towards every living thing, yet to have been the agent of destruction of tens of thousands of men; to have been inclined toward inaction, yet driven to action with unfathomable results; to recognize the incipient danger of power, yet directing the fate of millions of people.

Because of the author's thoroughness and his technique of amassing detail, Lincoln emerges as a highly complex figure. If there is evidence of idol worship, there is at the same time little attempt to hide the hero's flaws. If at the beginning Lincoln is shown as confused, he rises through humility to an almost dazzling statesmanship. If he is shrewd, he is also kindly, tolerant, forbearing to the point of saintliness (as witness his changing attitude toward his wife). If as politician he exercises virtual dictatorial power, he is seen to have been nevertheless merciful, actually benign. If at times he appears rough in his humor, it is ultimately a humor that cleanses, that relieves intolerable tensions.

In the chapter on "Lincoln's Laughter and Religion" (Chapter 56) Sandburg recounts anecdotes apparently without order or plan. When the reader considers what has preceded this chapter, however, and relates it to what follows, he can see its purpose. It comes between the accounts of the campaign of 1864 and of the election day—a period of high feeling and taut nerves. Though there is no attempt to picture Lincoln as a faithful proponent of organized religion, it is quite obvious that his basic temper was colored by an unshakable belief in an Ultimate Being. He found laughter and religion highly compatible, for a strong vein of confident mysticism wielded an influence on his emotion, thought, and action. The confidence of faith is akin to cosmic happiness—to optimism that produces laughter.

The opening chapters of Volume I picture with minute detail the confusion, the lack of direction, not only of the people but of their newly elected leader himself. The panoramic pattern is drawn by piling up phrases connected by semicolons. As the great narrative unfolds, the vilification of the President increases; the newspaper editors of the opposition grow vicious. All of Lincoln's prairie traits are turned against him: his lack of education, his country-boy gawkiness, his irrepressibly playful speech.

But by the time the reader has reached the final pages of Volume IV, he has been witness to a slow but sure change. With almost clinical particulars, Sandburg paints John Wilkes Booth's conspiracy to kill the President; the way Booth had been influenced by the opinions of men in high positions who saw Lincoln as clown, liar, and possibly monster; the assassination itself; and at the end the country's genuine mourning, strong testimony that the victim had at last overcome his obstacles, had indeed become a true martyr in the eyes of his countrymen. As for democracy itself, by the end of *The War Years* it is seen to have survived and worked and to have surmounted evil, ineptitude, hostility, and fearful mistakes. Despite the tragic end Sandburg transmits a sense of hope and trust in the concepts of democratic government.

What of the author and his attitude? What were his techniques and devices? First of all, it was obvious that Sandburg was a through-and-through American and that he had identified himself completely with his subject. His deep firsthand knowledge of the Middle West of Lincoln let him speak with assurance. He possessed an irresistible urge to tell his story and also the endurance to work patiently, prodigiously. His total absorption in the central figure of Lincoln let him speak with love. He needed never to raise his voice above normal as he once had, especially in some of his early poems. In fact, he was sometimes sunk in introspective reverie about this hero of the people. He shared, entered into, Lincoln's penetrating, astute, but tender regard for the common folk.

He was the right man at the right time from the right place concerned with the right subject to meet with consummate success. Like Lincoln, he was an earthy Midwesterner, a people's man, with poetic and narrative talent. In these four volumes he had found and presented the materials that were nearest to his heart and most suitable for his abilities.

The story of the four years moves, one must say, majestically. Never is there any sign of hurry or nervous telescoping. Sandburg explored all the byways and tributaries that led into any incident he was treating. The reader cannot complain of paucity of detail, for the account is exact and full. The author turned his attention in every possible way to the problems and the people Lincoln met daily. He gave in minute detail Lincoln's words and movements. He reported *verbatim* the comments of Lincoln's contemporaries about their President. This method was particularly appropriate to the materials and to the subject himself. Though not so even and consistent as Boswell on Johnson, Sandburg on Lincoln was richer and more varied. The slow movement and the piling up of minutiae in *The People, Yes* had here achieved the same ultimate sense of impact.

Second, the style of *The War Years* is an improvement over that of *The Prairie Years*. Besides the faithful reporting of all available details, Sandburg turned occasionally to a prose poetry which was sometimes emotionally profound; sometimes, however, it was less so—almost pretentious and inflated. These moments of lyric flights were spaced farther apart than in *The Prairie Years*, but they did permit Sandburg to let his imagination play over the facts of the record. One of the best such outbursts of lyricism occurred at the end of the chapter on the Gettysburg speech (Chapter 44).

> In many a country cottage over the land, a tall old clock in a quiet corner told time in a tick-tock deliberation. Whether the orchard branches hung with pink-spray blossoms or icicles of sleet, whether the outside news was seedtime or harvest, rain or drouth, births or deaths, the swing of the pendulum was right and left right and left in a tick-tock of deliberation.
>
> .   .   .   .
>
> To the backward and forward pendulum of a tall old clock in a quiet corner they might read those cadenced words while outside the windows the first flurry of snow blew across the orchard and down over the meadow, the beginnings of winter in a gun-metal gloaming to be later arched with a star-flung sky.

Another came at the conclusion of the entire work, after Booth had fired the fatal shot (Chapter 76).

> The ground lay white with appleblossoms this April week. The redbird whistled. Through black branches shone blue sky. Ships

put out from port with white sails catching the wind. Farmers spoke to their horses and turned furrows till sundown on the cornfield. Boys drew circles in cinder paths and played marbles. Lilac bushes took on surprises of sweet, light purple. In many a back yard the potato-planting was over. In this house was a wedding, in that one a new-born baby, in another a girl with a new betrothal ring. Life went on. Everywhere life went on.

.   .   .   .

Evergreen carpeted the stone floor of the vault. On the coffin set in a receptacle of black walnut they arranged flowers carefully and precisely, they poured flowers as symbols, they lavished heaps of fresh flowers as though there could never be enough to tell either their hearts or his.

And then night came with great quiet.

And there was rest.

The prairie years, the war years, were over.

These last chapters recreated the elegiac mood of the entire North. Though the inevitable intensity of feeling was never absent, the people involved seemed to be moving in a dream; for Sandburg's language was subdued, his attitude was reverent. This restraint, the control of materials and mood, could have been achieved only by a writer in complete possession of his subject matter, not only through long and intimate association with the sources, but through the very life he had led from the beginning.

Sandburg's basic method, then, as it had been in *The People, Yes* and to a great degree in *The Prairie Years,* was the amassing of detail; and the result seems at first quick glance to be without any selection, just sheer mass. A patient study, however, shows the cumulative power of this concrete stockpiling. Step by step, stroke by stroke, Sandburg had created a reliable impression of the Civil War period as well as of the figure at the center—patient, growing, at last overcoming, and then himself overcome by death. It is hard to believe that Sandburg had not produced a portrait of the total Lincoln.

The author had apparently adopted no thesis; he had no ax to grind. Except that his patent admiration for Lincoln showed through in every sentence, he wrote with no prominent points of emphasis, but with a newsman's clarity, not attempting analysis, but letting interpretation remain implicit. The details were all free and equal, not forced into a Procrustean

CARL SANDBURG

bed, lopped and distorted to support an argument. In the midst
of the generally short chapters (such had been the nature of the
numerous details), the author could present one like Chapter
40 which is the length of an ordinary book, on patterns of living and activity in the White House without losing his pace or
the interest of a sympathetic reader.

Though his details were precise, his language, except for the
rare lyric passages, did not have the precious sheen of a highly
polished craft. Instead, there was the same careful avoidance
of drawing-room elegance, the same dedication to the language
of the people that had marked *Chicago Poems*. Elegance in the
early poems, if that was what it was, came from a thoughtful
and conscientious selection of the right word for the right place.
The effect of *The War Years* depended on the fact that it was an
American book, as American as Mark Twain. It was as American, indeed, as a moving picture; for in summoning witnesses,
in lining up incidents, in sifting gossip, in gathering the evidence, Sandburg had moved from place to place, from rumor to
rumor, from figure to figure, with the ease of a skillful, artful, but
apparently unhurried cameraman.

The mass of detail served an ultimately excellent purpose, but
one could nevertheless wish for somewhat more concentration,
selection, contraction. The tiny incidental gesture received the
same loving care and attention as the momentous episode. The
very democratic view that everything deserves as finely drawn
a presentation as everything else had sacrificed any perspective.
One could wish occasionally for less minor fact and more
opinion from the author himself. The Sumter question (Chapter
7) was treated at length and with elaboration; but Sandburg
had not weighed conflicting testimony as to whether the President's decision was intended to be provocative or not.

The method of piling example on example was for many
readers superfluous and top-heavy. In the act of showing Lincoln's slow growth, Sandburg had drawn in too much really
irrelevant material. It is indeed difficult to see the principle
involved in devoting less space to the three days of the Battle
of Gettysburg (fifteen pages) than to the tributes—however
emotionally sincere and widespread—after the shooting of the
President (thirty-one pages).

Despite the drawbacks of mountainous details, though, one

must admit that they are not cluttered; they are presented in meticulous order. And despite a feeling that Sandburg had treated all points equally and that all too often the sentences read like notes and the chapters like scrapbooks of clippings, one must admit that, possibly through this very richness of detail, the author had sustained suspense through many pages: as, for example, at the beginning of the story (Chapter 2,), in the recounting of the eleven-day journey from Springfield through Baltimore to Washington before the first Inauguration, in the communication of the nervous anxiety of office-seekers (Chapter 6), and in the telling of the nearly unbearable tensions of the Election Day of 1864 (Chapter 58).

Though Sandburg's sense of language had not always prevented him from yielding to such clichés as "the seven seas," "checkered domain," or "rolling prairies," yet his flair for the apt phrase was a frequent reminder that here was a poet at work. He said that Stanton "knew the Constitution and the price of eggs and was solemn about both" (Chapter 18) and that Sumner "sprawled in puddles of the ridiculous and the asinine" (Chapter 62). Occasional flashes like these enlivened the facts.

Another characteristic of the narrative he had brought over from *The Prairie Years*. It was for the most part confined within a frame of contemporaneity. As if he were writing a novel, Sandburg did not give away the outcome. Men were shown speculating as to whether or not Congress would ratify Lincoln's election. The false alarms, the indecisions, the cares and fears at the opening of the hostilities were made real and full of suspense by the technique of refraining from disclosing even a hint of the future. In spite of the historian's inevitable foreknowledge of the end result, Sandburg had created the illusion of life—had made his story dynamic by refusing to suggest anything of events to come.

These four volumes did not add up simply to the story of the life of a single man; they were just as clearly a story of the folk. Battle tactics and Congressional action were noted, but greater attention went to picturing men and women. All sorts of people were brought on the stage, dismissed, summoned again. They were talked about, they were looked at with varying degrees of intensity. Sometimes the portraits were miniatures, sometimes they were life-size, but they had flesh and blood. It was in these—the pocket biographies—that Sandburg was at his creative best. The reader was brought into the presence of Charles Sumner, Thaddeus Stevens, Horace Greeley, Jefferson Davis, Robert E. Lee—the list is very long indeed. Hundreds of individuals were involved, some of them even only slightly. The entire work amounted to a panoramic history of a whole people; but always at the center was Lincoln. In the midst of detailing social and political history, stood, walked, sat, slept, ate, and talked the towering figure whom Sandburg adored.

Though the professional historians[4] expressed dissatisfaction with Sandburg's passing over much unpublished manuscript material and many scholarly monographs, the reader must be impressed, even if bored, by the minutiae. He is sometimes moved by the emotional involvement and consequent lyricism of the author. He can recognize the often saving humor. But he senses above all Sandburg's admiration for his subject and the way it had taken him—not in the direction of a blind lover's exaggeration or distortion, but toward simple, honest reporting that resulted in breadth, humaneness, and drama.

CHAPTER 7

Harvest Years

I *Politics and Patriotism*

POLITICIANS now began to consider Carl Sandburg as a possible candidate for office. Rumors got about that he might be nominated for Congress (President Roosevelt wrote him a note on May 29, 1940, to say his "kind of Lincoln liberal" would be welcome in Washington);[1] Republicans began to wonder if he could beat Roosevelt in the race for the Presidency. This suggestion he declined, for he may have been an independent voter, but he favored the Democratic platform over the Republican. In fact, as early as 1933, he had supported the New Deal to such an extent that Robert Frost expressed a disapproval that persisted long afterwards. During Roosevelt's 1940 campaign Sandburg supported the New Deal cause. He took to the road lecturing against the European dictatorships. The title of his speech was "What Lincoln Would Have Done." The gist of his message was that his hero—and the great folk hero of the American people—would have done exactly what Roosevelt was doing. He continued his public support of the President even after his fourth inauguration. In June, 1941, he spoke in Yankee Stadium, New York, praising Roosevelt's stand against Germany. He stressed one of his recurrent themes: "The future is beyond any man's reading. We are moving into an adventure beyond the horizon, and I am taking my chances with those who say 'God bless the President of the United States.'"[2]

In spite of his support of Roosevelt, Sandburg still insisted that he was not a member of any political party. He was, however, a member of many organizations related to his life and work. Harvard had elected him to Phi Beta Kappa in 1928. He had been elected a member of the National Institute of Arts and

Letters, and in November, 1940, he had been chosen for the élite circle, the American Academy of Arts and Letters. Various writers' groups attracted him: the Authors' League of America, the Michigan Authors' Association, and the National Press Club of Washington. He belonged to two veterans' organizations: the Spanish-American War Veterans and the Veterans of Foreign Wars, which he once served as historian. He also belonged to the Friends of Our Native Landscape and to the American Milk Goat Record Association. Of Lutheran heritage, he had not, however, aligned himself with any organized religious group, though from time to time he had indicated that he might be harboring faith in a Creator.

In Michigan, Clare Hoffman of the House of Representatives at Washington was an ultraconservative, the arch-enemy of labor unions. Conscious of Sandburg's sympathy for labor and of his popularity as a writer about the common man, in 1942 the members of the Democratic political machine privately asked him to run against Hoffman. Again he had to refuse. In order to avoid any public embarrassment, he sent a quiet message to the headquarters of the United Auto Workers saying that for several reasons he had better remain a private citizen rather than enter politics formally.

He was still replying to questions about *The War Years*. In explaining his reportorial method, he had said that he "would rather have a good photograph, that had not been monkeyed with, that had clear, definite lines, than an interpretive painting by anyone. And I would rather make the good photograph in words in a biographical work. . . ." [3] He admired his photographer brother-in-law Edward Steichen so much that he was trying to emulate him. He was glad that he had waited to write *The War Years* until his capacity for judgment was mature: "I completely rewrote the notes I had set down on two members of Lincoln's cabinet—Chase and Seward. I understood them, as I had not when I was a younger man." In general, he felt the need to accomplish three things by his work: "to write the books that I most wanted when I was a boy"; "to make full use of the American speech"; and "to prick a bubble here and there, to point out now and again the men who don't know as much as they think they know."

His pen was still busy. In the spring of 1941 before America's outright entry into World War II, he had composed and recited on sound track the commentaries for two documentary films for the government: one on the country's air power and the other on the New Deal's controversial Tennessee Valley Authority project. Then after December 7, he was caught up in the effort to win the war. He did not believe in violence between wars, he had said; but when violence was inevitable to defeat an enemy he would support it. In 1942 Harcourt, Brace brought out selections from *The War Years* under the title *Storm over the Land*. The following year appeared *Home Front Memo,* a miscellaneous collection of broadcasts, speeches, pamphlets, legends, poems, and newspaper columns. (He had been writing for the Chicago *Daily Times* syndicate since the beginning of the war.) At New York's Museum of Modern Art, Steichen had arranged an exhibit of photographs called "Road to Victory," with captions by Sandburg. These were reproduced also in *Home Front Memo.* Sandburg's great patriotism was abundantly evident.

In 1945, soon after peace had been declared, the Sandburgs moved from their home on the Michigan dunes to "Connemara," a farm near Flat Rock, North Carolina, where the temperatures would be milder in the winters. They shipped the goats by express, packed up all the Lincoln materials and other books and the furniture, and left the Midwest as a residence for the first time. Sandburg himself was sixty-seven; so it was not likely that the Midwest in him would be dissipated in this Southern atmosphere.

The following year, on the ninetieth anniversary of the Lincoln-Douglas Debate at Knox College, October 7, 1946, Sandburg's birthplace was dedicated as a museum. A large Lincoln Room had been added to the original three small rooms to house Sandburg's books and various appropriate memorabilia. That the author had lived there only a very short time as a baby made no difference. Now admirers would be provided with a point of focus for their hero worship. School children had contributed thousands of Lincoln pennies for the restoration of the little building, and they have continued to help with the cost of upkeep.

II   *Remembrance Rock*

On June 11, 1944, the New York *Times* (II, 3) had carried the announcement that Sandburg had signed a contract with Metro-Goldwyn-Mayer for "a biographical novel of American life, manners, and morals." It would be called *An American Cavalcade*. The idea of a "great American novel" was, of course, not new. In 1928 he had planned just such a book, but his energies had been diverted by the success of *The Prairie Years* and by his growing absorption in his Lincoln research. The four volumes of *The War Years* now behind him, he was free to devote his time and efforts elsewhere. World War II had returned him briefly to journalism, but, after he had signed the contract with Metro-Goldwyn-Mayer, he went right to work on the novel and published no new books for four years until he had completed the lengthy manuscript. At the time of the book's appearance he explained that the topic of America was so big as to deserve a book twice as long. Only his age had prevented him from expanding the work. During the course of composition he had thought of giving it the title of *The Angel of the Backward Look*, a phrase he had found in the journals of William Bradford of the Plymouth Colony. He and his publishers decided against this name, however, because of its close resemblance to Thomas Wolfe's *Look Homeward, Angel*. They settled on *Remembrance Rock*.[4]

The structure of the book is plain: prologue, three parts, and epilogue. The prologue takes place in Washington, where Orville Brand Windom, a former Justice of the Supreme Court, is waiting out World War II with his daughter-in-law Maria and his grandson, Joseph Stilwell Windom. In the front yard of his home is a large boulder, "Remembrance Rock," under which he has buried earth from Plymouth, Valley Forge, Gettysburg, and the Argonne Forest. As a speaker (he addresses a national radio audience) he shows himself to be much like Sandburg himself— liberal, knowledgeable about American history, often vague, and even sentimental. As conversationalist the Justice is made by the author to depart altogether from life and to talk as not even a self-conscious and tiresome pedant would talk (no matter how he would write). In Chapter 2 he says: "The finest of our precision watches, the most supercolossal of our supercargo planes, don't compare with a newborn baby in the number and ingenuity of coils and springs, in the flow and change of chemical solutions, in timing devices and interrelated parts that are irreplaceable." This sentence is hardly the spontaneous stuff of dialogue with one's daughter-in-law. For a man of great fascination with the American speech habits, Sandburg had no ear for natural conversation. His assiduous collecting of slang, proverbs, and informal anecdotes had not helped him in original imaginative dialogue. The Justice dies soon after his national broadcast. His grandson, Captain Raymond Windom, returns from Okinawa and finds a "novel" in a locked box—three stories the Justice has written that are parallel in character, situation, and intention—to testify to the validity of the American Dream. All three stories come to the conclusion that the crises they detail have left America a finer nation. This novel within a novel, the Justice explains in a note, is his legacy to Raymond, Maria, and their son, Joseph Stilwell Windom.

The time of the opening of the first story is 1608; the place, Scrooby, England. Oliver Ball Windrow, a woodcarver, makes a small bronze plaque on which he inscribes the Four Stumbling Blocks to Truth first listed by Roger Bacon:

1. The influence of fragile or unworthy authority.
2. Custom.
3. The imperfection of undisciplined senses.
4. Concealment of ignorance by ostentation of seeming wisdom.

Having hung the plaque on a silver cord, he presents it to young Mary Windling, of a Separatist family. He is in love with her, but she chooses instead to marry a boy nearer her own age, John Spong. Windrow is a man of philosophic bent, one half of his face showing a dreaminess, the other half wrath; he is an interesting man, but simply too old for Mary. The Spongs join the Separatist group that goes to Leyden, Holland, where they live for twelve years. When she receives the news that Windrow has died, Mary is touched with sadness; but her sorrow is made lighter by the exciting plans of the Pilgrims to go to the New World. She and John and their little daughter, Remember, are on the *Mayflower* as it sails from Plymouth in 1620. Remember carries with her the memory of a boy driving off other boys who were tormenting her on the wharf before the ship sails.

In the first harsh winter on New England shores, Mary dies, leaving to Remember the bronze plaque Windrow had made. The years pass, and Remember grows up in Plymouth, strong and quite independent. John Spong gradually becomes gloomy and uncommunicative. When Orton Wingate begins to come frequently to the house to see Remember, John is suspicious. Orton's face is considerably like Windrow's, half peaceful, half stormy. As her mother had rejected Windrow, so Remember rejects Wingate, just as she refuses a proposal from a transient sailor who, though possessed of a wild past, straightens up temporarily while in Plymouth. Remember, who has a mind of her own, is not afraid to befriend a town drunkard; but when Roger Williams comes to town, she fears to listen to his sermons because he makes her realize her own comparatively free-thinking propensities, heresy in this strictly Calvinist community.

In 1638, a young man named Resolved Wayfare follows Williams into Plymouth, for he is determined to find out for himself just what this man stands for. Wayfare proves to be the boy who had protected Remember on the Plymouth wharf in England eighteen years before. Though he saves John Spong's life during a devastating blizzard and otherwise shows himself to be a responsible person, he cannot convince Remember that she should join him in helping to establish Roger Williams's settlement on Narragansett Bay, for she continues to follow her father's strict belief that Williams's liberal attitude towards religious faith is a gift straight from the Devil. When Wayfare leaves the Plymouth colony, he and Remember look toward the future. They have a feeling they will meet again. As a kind of surety, Remember gives Resolved Wayfare the Bacon plaque she has inherited from her mother.

The second story takes place during the Revolutionary War. Ordway Winshore is on his way to New York and Boston to see his sons, both of whom have followed their father in the printing business. Winshore, a master printer in Philadelphia, has the facial characteristics of Windrow and Wingate—half peace, half wrath. Two of his companions in the coach headed north are two brothers, Francis and George Frame, both lieutenants in the

British army. The time is March, 1775. Feeling is running high. When Francis Frame breaks his hand in striking a man who has dared to curse George III, Winshore recognizes that war is inevitable. In New York, where Winshore has a two-day visit with his typesetter son (John) Locke, he learns that his other son, Robert, is active in Massachusetts in the cause of independence. Robert also is paying court to an assistant seamstress in a dressmaker's shop.

As he continues his journey to Boston, Winshore finds himself once again in the company of the Frame brothers. George Frame amuses himself by a flirtation with another passenger, Marintha Wilming, who is, unknown to Winshore, the seamstress whom Robert has been paying attention to. In the Boston shop where Marintha (Mim) works there is gossip about the false marriage by which a British sergeant has seduced an innocent girl, Ann Elwood. It is now that Winshore learns of Robert's attachment to Mim; he goes to call on her at her aunt's house. One day in a bookstore he meets Mary Burton, whom he as a widower is soon to marry and take with him back to Philadelphia. Outside Boston Robert, in his zeal for independence, has helped to tar and feather a well-to-do Tory named Reggs for informing on a British deserter. The man's daughter, Sapphira, has witnessed the punishment, and at the dressmaker's shop she recognizes Robert, who manages to escape when George Frame attempts to arrest him. In the scuffle and excitement, however, Robert loses the bronze Bacon plaque, which he has inherited from a great-granduncle.

At the Battle of Lexington Mim's brother is killed and George Frame is permanently crippled. When Robert slips back into Boston to report these things to Mim, she turns away, unwilling to forgive him for the part he has played in the rebellion and violence. Robert's adventures continue. When with Oates Elwood, brother to the betrayed Ann, he is on his way to Quebec with Benedict Arnold, both he and Elwood are stricken with illness. Later, after the evacuation, Robert is brought back to Boston for convalescence. He shows up at the Continental Congress in Philadelphia. His brother Locke and Oates Elwood hurry through town on their way to deliver messages to George Washington. Locke is killed the next night. He has not had time to report that he has married Ann Elwood in secret. Mim

Wilming, now employed in a dress shop in Philadelphia, delivers Locke's shroud. When confronted with Robert, she at last forgives him, for she now sees the justice in the cause of the revolutionists.

In the year of the Declaration of Independence, Ann gives birth to a son, whom she names after his dead father, Locke. No longer making dresses, Mim is nursing the sick and wounded at Bethlehem. When word reaches Philadelphia that she is ill, Ordway Winshore in disguise braves the British lines to bring her home. Robert dies at Valley Forge. Mim then shows his father the Bacon plaque, which she has found months before, after Robert's flight from Boston. Ordway tells her she should keep the plaque. After the British leave Philadelphia, Oates Elwood arrives with his sister Ann and her baby, Locke's son. This child represents the future to them. He is a figure in the American Dream.

The third story begins sixty years later, in 1836. Omri Winwold has been leading a seemingly aimless life. Like earlier characters in the novel, he has a face half calm, half turbulent. Having married a woman of promiscuous tendencies, he becomes father of a son named Andrew Marvel. He decides to head for the West (Indiana or Illinois). On the way he stops to say goodbye to a distant cousin in Arpa, New York. The cousin, Brooksany (Brooks) Wimbler, has had sympathy for his unconventional ways and his apparently goalless life. Her husband Joel, a harness maker, is quite the opposite of Omri; he is a steady citizen and an abolitionist. Omri's wife Bee is unfaithful just once too many times; so he takes his son Andrew and disappears, the Wimblers suppose to the West, since he has spoken so much of the opportunities over the Alleghenies. The Wimblers themselves catch the spirit of the westward movement. They take their little girl Millicent (Mibs) out to Illinois, where they help to establish the community of New Era (near Galesburg). The general temper of the town is strongly antislavery.

As Mibs grows up, she attracts the attention of various young men. Two ardent admirers in particular she refuses to marry, one of whom is Hornsby Meadows, a supporter of the abolitionist cause and an instructor at the college in New Era. He finally marries another teacher. Without her parents' consent,

Mibs marries Rodney Wayman, a Southerner who has drifted into town.

Meanwhile, Omri Winwold has indeed come west. In Pike County he has done well. Though he does not know the whereabouts of Bee, he takes a chance on bigamy and marries Sarah Prindle and then, after Sarah's death, her sister. By 1857 he has had eight children by three wives. Earlier, in St. Louis, he has seen Bee and her new husband, Henry Flack. True to form, Bee runs away from Flack. At the death of his third wife, Omri becomes fast friends with Flack.

Rodney Wayman brings his bride, Mibs Wimbler, to the town of Atlas, where Wayman is well known as a cattle buyer. When she sees Omri, Mibs realizes that she is his distant cousin and tells him that her mother is in New Era. Omri renews relationships with Brooks through exchange of letters. Just a few months before Lincoln is elected President, Wayman and Mibs become the parents of a baby boy, whom they name Clayborn Joel Wayman. Then the Civil War breaks out. Southerner that he is, Wayman goes to Texas, where he and his friend Nack Doss become captains in the Confederate Army. His friend is killed and Wayman is taken prisoner, but he effects an escape.

In the first year of the war Mibs gives birth to another son, Rodney, Jr. Her father, home from the war, dies in New Era; and only a few days later, his wife Brooksany dies also. Among their belongings Mibs finds the Bacon plaque, which she begins to wear around her neck. Her husband, again taken prisoner, is lying near Fredericksburg in a barn turned hospital. Next to him is Colonel Hornsby Meadows, one of Mibs's New Era suitors. Meadows dies; Mibs gets through the enemy lines and, in an exchange of prisoners, brings Rodney back to Illinois. One evening at supper with Omri Winwold, Wayman sees Omri's sons, who were crippled in the War fighting on the side of the Union. Their sacrifice softens his heart, and he loses his bitterness. The third story ends in 1865. Though the War is over, the country is grief-stricken by the assassination of the President. Mibs, however, sees the great virtue in the preservation of the Union and is profoundly glad. The American Dream can move on toward fulfillment.

The epilogue returns the scene to Washington after the death of Justice Windom in 1945. Captain Raymond Windom and his wife Maria have read the three stories that the Justice has left to posterity. They recognize that their own time, no less than the periods of the novel, has been a time of crisis for the United States; but they know that the country has come through again and is still searching for even richer fulfillment of the American Dream of a place of freedom for all its peoples. Following the elder Windom's example, they bury beneath Remembrance Rock gravel from Anzio Beach, sand from Utah Beach in Normandy, and a block of volcanic ash from Okinawa.

* * *

On this outline hang the words of Carl Sandburg. The book is hard to categorize, for its final effect is one of a prolonged chanting about the greatness, the religion, the ineffable mystique of America. That Sandburg loves his America there can be not the slightest doubt. He is sincere, generous, and uninhibited as he records local scene, local customs, local speech habits, folklore of all sorts. If one can condense a theme from this sprawling material, it is the necessity for tolerance, the rooting out of bigotry to come eventually with the American goal of individual freedom and self-realization. As a link reminding the reader of the central idea, the little bronze plaque bearing Bacon's Four Stumbling Blocks to Freedom appears in each of the three historical sections. Sandburg is trying to show his readers that the way forward is based in the past. If America's present is in disorder, the blame may partially be laid at the door of ignorance of history.

When one tries to see relation between form and meaning, he realizes that the author has been attempting to show how really very casual are the life patterns, how diffusive are the substances from which national crises grow and from which, to be specific, America has emerged at the same time powerful and democratic. To achieve this result, Sandburg obviously did a great deal of digging into history, for the detail in each of the parts is overwhelming.

Unfortunately, the product of all this industriousness is static. There is no flow. There is only Sandburg's wandering about amidst the vastnesses of American folklore. In attempting to give individuating traits to the faceless masses of *The People, Yes,* in this novel he has put on display wooden figures in an over-full showcase. With an eye to the continuum, he has resorted to repetition of facial characteristics, for example, that can be labeled only a device of stilted allegory: Oliver Ball Windrow and Orton Wingate of the Plymouth episodes, Ordway Winshore of the Revolutionary period, and Omri Winwold of the Civil War era all have faces alike—one side marked by peace and the other by wrath, conflict, doom. (The Bacon plaque, of course, is intended to hold the parts of the novel together, also.)

The coincidence of initials and even syllables in the names of the principal male characters of each story may have been intended to contribute to coherence, but it could conceivably be a source of unnecessary confusion: Oliver Ball Windrow, Orville Brand Windom, Orton Wingate, Ordway Winshore, Omri Winwold; Roger Williams, Resolved Wayfare, Robert Winshore, Rodney Wayman, Raymond Windom. Not only the men but the women too are given similar names: Mary Windling, Marintha ("Mim") Wilming, Millicent ("Mibs") Wimbler, and Maria ("Mimah") Windom. The trick is artificial. As the men tend to look alike in the three periods, the girls they associate with have dancing feet and are possessed of those traits which add up to "all woman." The final effect is one of puppets, not of flesh-and-blood human beings out of our country's past.

The 1,067 pages are packed with detail—songs, proverbs, anecdotes, folk customs—a pattern familiar to the Sandburg reader. The author, who could not resist his own inclination toward lyric tangents, often assigned long speeches in poetic prose that are totally unsuitable to the characters. The conversations are in a vein that common sense would say the speakers are incapable of. At the other extreme, he has his people speaking to each other in earthy maxims and folk proverbs too unnatural for realistic dialogue. He is still cataloguing wisdom as in *The People, Yes.*

Whole sections of the papers of Winthrop and Bradford, quoted word for word, fill up the wooden dialogue of the characters. A letter of Roger Williams and the Declaration of Independence are printed as if they were free verse, a liberty Sandburg had taken with the words of Lincoln in *The People, Yes.* If this device proves anything at all, it is that he recognizes the natural rhythmic quality of these documents as resembling his own. The fact remains that they were written as prose, and the judgment must be that to present them in any other way is distortion.

The action moves slowly, painfully so, because of the lists and the digressions that are invaluable to the historian but need to be digested and used more succinctly, compactly, and imaginatively in a novel. The long roster of the Pilgrim Fathers does not help the action. The accounts of the Pilgrims' business and political relations with the Indians are drawn from important chapters in American history, but these recitals retard the pace of the plot almost to the point of absolute standstill. It is true that not every moment in life is tense and dramatic, but in art one expects to find a distillation of the life experience, and not a plodding, faithful record of every gesticulation. Even in a fiction "faithful" to everyday life one finds selection and direction.

Sandburg's attempts at philosophic depth and his slow-moving dignity are broken through now and then by incidents lively in content if not in the telling. Sometimes the material is lurid, sometimes dramatic without appeal to lust; but too often for unity's sake it is irrelevant to the stream of the story. The tarring and feathering of Sapphira Regg's father, the heated love affairs between soldiers and their women, who are faithful and patient (as women should be!), the taking of spies—all have the potential of excitement and absorbing movement, but they simply add in a vague way to the variegated background out of which America had emerged by 1945, the time the novel closes. The main narrative has to wait until these incidents are told before it can proceed with the business at hand.

The problem was closely related to Sandburg's ardor, which overrode any profound thinking through. So enthusiastic and patriotic an American was he, that he idealized his feelings about democracy to the point of unreality. Resonant, grave, even priestly, he needed a sense of humor to give a true picture of his country; for even the jokes were tacked on, not integrated into the style or the tone.

Of the Justice's three stories, the section on the Pilgrim Fathers has the best direction because the matters at stake during the seventeenth century were simpler and clearer. The plot grows from the patent bravery of the Pilgrims as they come to America, moves through intolerance and resultant cruelty as they try to maintain what they consider the *status quo* of their little settlement, and ends on a favorite Sandburg note of anti-bigotry with the influence of Roger Williams and the breaching of the barrier against true religious freedom.

In the next section Sandburg recognized the doubts about the American cause against the British and the unwillingness of many men of honor to become entangled in so desperate an action. The chances of success for the colonists he pointed out as slim; the almost superhuman endurance of the army at Valley Forge he italicized as more than heroic. He was working on the thesis of how stupendous an obligation contemporary America owes the men of the Revolutionary period.

The Civil War years being more complex, Sandburg was nevertheless working with materials that he had known thoroughly and for a long time. He found in the abolitionists the same kind of cruelty that had manifested itself in the Pilgrims—a cruelty based on the ignoring of tolerance and human dignity. (The abolitionists did not see in their own backyard the bestiality in the mills of New England.) Sandburg played his searchlight on the butchery of the Civil War, in spite of which the States remained a Union. One finds emphasis on the common man—the stories of the abolitionists, incidents of the underground railway, the flourishing of the people on the Illinois prairie land around Galesburg—points of focus springing from the author's early enthusiasm for the Populist movement and the cause of the Social-Democrats.

It is Populism that filled the book with jokes irrelevant to the mainstream, popular songs dragged in for "color," historical information intended to give authenticity to the narrative. Though the ultimate purpose of civilization is to develop man and his environment to that high point which can be expressed, ironically, only in axioms and proverbs, such clichés do not make engrossing reading in themselves. Furthermore, trite phrases, no matter how universally true, do not apply to America any more than to any other country that aims at freedom and tolerance. One cannot find anything peculiarly American about the concept that the people are always with us or that life will not be stamped out even though individuals leave the scene.

Just as the pattern is too neat in broad outline and too loose in detail, so the language itself is troublesome—the mixture the author had been using from the beginning: passing slang, normal diction, saccharine sentimentality, apocalyptic turgidity. The habit of inverting normal sentence order becomes noticeably eccentric. The belaboring of symbols (the almost embarrassingly coincidental reappearance of the Bacon plaque, for example) is artificial and unbelievable. The lengthy and much too frequent direct quotation of undigested materials out of the documents of the American past is tiresome and slow.

What one finds often in Sandburg's poetry, he finds in this novel—vague affirmation of democratic principles, definite optimism about America's future, dedication to the cause of unity in society, the anonymous piling up of persons and things on which America's strength depends. One must admit that the concept of the novel is commendable. One must admit to Sandburg's benevolence and freedom from bigotry. But one cannot find evidence of ability to control materials in such a way as to produce a work of art.

The reviewers for the most part were disappointed. [5] Diana Trilling went so far as to say that the book was not worth reviewing. Sandburg was angry with her, although he said that what the critics found or did not find in his work was of no consequence to him. Apparently unaware of Sandburg's contract with Metro-Goldwyn-Mayer, Perry Miller saw the novel as a script for a Hollywood spectacular. He could visualize how three astronomically salaried stars could be cast in the three principal roles in each of the four periods, with only costumes, century, and scenery as the chief changes. All the ingredients were present for a mass-appeal moving picture: gory battles, sexual encounters, and what would pass for tender feeling.

In 1926, when he reviewed *The Prairie Years* in *The Bookman*, [6] John Farrar had said: "I am convinced that Carl Sandburg could be the supreme American novelist of his period. He has the depth of a Dreiser, combined with a stronger grasp of broad aspects of human character and a limpid, graphic style." In 1948, as it turned out, *Remembrance Rock* had not succeeded. The organization was too wooden, the story was too disconnected, the modes of coherence were too artificial, and the characters were too allegorical for even Hollywood to work with. Metro-Goldwyn-Mayer has never attempted to put the novel on the screen.

III *Honors and Awards*

The long task of writing his novel was now over, but Sandburg was not one to sit for long in an easy chair. As a matter of fact, during the last months of seeing the book through the press, he had found time to lend his name and talents to other projects. In January, 1948, he had accepted the honorary chairmanship of the Midwest "Freedom Train," which would collect food for postwar Europe. He had made a fifteen-minute speech in Springfield, Illinois, at the inauguration of Governor Adlai Stevenson, whom he had long admired. He had contributed a chapter to an elaborately planned *Literary History of the United States.* [7] His essay on his hero as a man of letters ("Abraham Lincoln: The Soil and the Seed") was typical Sandburg, despite the efforts of the editors to bring the style more into line with the rest of the book. In 1949 he published *Lincoln Collector,* a description of the Lincolniana in the collection of his lawyer friend Oliver R. Barrett. It is of interest to history scholars for its account and reproductions of pictures and manuscripts.

In 1950 Broadcast Music, Inc., of New York published a *New American Songbag,* printing again about forty of the songs from the original 1927 *Songbag* and adding many others. But the big event of this year was the publication of Sandburg's *Complete Poems.* To the six volumes published between 1916 and 1936 he added a "New Section" containing fifty-five pages of verses either new or excluded from earlier books for various reasons. Robert Sherwood in the New York *Herald-Tribune* and Henry Commager in the *Times* took ample space for a summing up of the poet's accomplishment. [8] Even discounting his inevitably uninspired, even unpalatable pieces, Sandburg was a major literary figure of the twentieth century and one still too close to critics for anything like final judgment. The *Complete Poems* brought him his second Pulitzer Prize. In April, 1952, he also accepted the gold medal for history from the American Academy of Arts and Letters. He was now without doubt a top-ranking, even though controversial, figure in American letters.

A writer hard to pigeon-hole, he had made an undeniable impression as a poet on the course of literature. If his language had been a departure from what had been expected, if it smacked of the streets and factories, it was nevertheless real American speech. If his tone was chiefly midwestern, it nevertheless transcended regional boundaries and entered the world of man's condition. If his subject matter was full of the exigencies of the machine age, he strove with a poet's will to see what beauty could be unearthed from the new materials. Even if not always successful, as a pioneer he had nevertheless been bold, imaginative, and compassionate.

Since 1904 Sandburg had been using a guitar to accompany his singing of folk songs. Now he undertook some lessons from Andres Segovia, the Spanish virtuoso. The master assigned the student some very difficult exercises, though how well he would come out only time could tell. Since Segovia and Sandburg had been friends for several years, the Spaniard could testify with authority to the basic joyfulness in his pupil's spirit. An elderly man in years, Sandburg still had the youthful energies and motivations to keep on experimenting, exploring, and learning.

On his seventy-fifth birthday, the day of publication for *Always the Young Strangers,* Sandburg was in Chicago, where Governor Stevenson had declared a "Carl Sandburg Day." The banquet for five hundred fifty people at the Blackstone was a glittering affair. Hundreds of his admirers had been disappointed at being turned away. Governor Stevenson addressed the gathering by radio. Among other ceremonies that night, Sandburg received at the hands of Erik Boheman, Swedish Ambassador to the United States, the Commanders Cup of the Royal Order of the North Star.

In this diamond jubilee year the Illinois State Historical Society published a special edition of its *Journal* (dated 1952) honoring its illustrious native son. Alfred Harcourt contributed an article on "Forty Years of Friendship"; Robert Sherwood recalled "A Cold Walk with Carl"; Frederick Hill Meserve revealed his "Thoughts on a Friend"; Governor Stevenson wrote as "A Friend and Admirer." The many tributes covered almost a hundred twenty-five pages.

On January 6, 1963, his publishers brought out another volume of poems by Sandburg, *Honey and Salt,* his first book of major proportions since 1953. Though he has been far from idle, Sandburg has deliberately slowed his pace. His works, however, have been translated into a number of foreign languages, including Chinese and Burmese. He has been the subject of scholarly studies in France, Denmark, and Sweden. Reprints and shortened editions have come to the bookstores: a one-volume life of Lincoln; *Prairie-Town Boy,* taken from *Always the Young Strangers; The Sandburg Range,* a survey of his entire career with a little new material; a selection from *Remembrance Rock* called *The Fiery Trial; Harvest Poems,* a small paperback collection from the *Complete Poems,* with a few additions; *Wind Song,* some of the old poems, with a few new ones intended for children.

He has written a few forewords and is now at work on the sequel to *Always the Young Strangers,* which begins with his entrance as a provisional freshman at Lombard at the age of twenty. He now, for the first time in his long career, has a formal agreement with an agent, Lucy Kroll, who arranges his radio and television engagements and finds a market for his current writing. In 1960 *Playboy* paid thirty-six hundred dollars for six poems and a parable which were published as a booklet by the University of Kentucky Press a few months after their appearance in the magazine.

In the past decade he has been on the Ed Sullivan Show, he has read his poems while Gene Kelly danced to them before the television cameras, he has stridden over the battlefields at Gettysburg talking with vigor and authority as the cameras followed him. His poems and prose have been the material for a widely successful stage production—*The World of Carl Sandburg*—under the direction of Norman Corwin, the lines spoken by Bette Davis and Gary Merrill, the songs sung by Clark Allen. In 1960 he went to Hollywood as adviser on the dialogue of *The Greatest Story Ever Told* for Twentieth-Century-Fox.

Prizes and honorary degrees have been showered on him. (When Ernest Hemingway won the Nobel Prize for Literature in 1954, he said that Sandburg deserved the honor more than he.) In June, 1955, he received the five-hundred-dollar prize in poetry at the Boston Arts Festival. Archibald MacLeish there praised him as the "poet of the American affirmation . . . singer of the city where no one before him thought song could be found, and the voice of a prairie country which had been silent until he came." [9] On April 16, 1956, he received the humanities award from the Albert Einstein College of Medicine of Yeshiva

University, New York. On the night of January 20, 1959, he received the Doctor of Letters degree from Upsala College in East Orange, New Jersey—ten years after it had been voted him. His work had prevented his attending the earlier ceremony.

In the summer of 1959 he was in Stockholm, having gone to Europe with Steichen for the opening of the photographic exhibit of "The Family of Man," for which he had written the captions. He was the center of a ten-day celebration. Before thousands at a Swedish-American Day program he read in Swedish his mother's last letter. A few days later he received from the hands of King Gustav VI the "Litteris et Artibus" award, an honor rarely accorded a foreigner.

His liberal views are still reflected in his public statements and acts. During the week-long celebration of "Chicago Dynamic" sponsored by the Chicago Association of Commerce and Industry in October, 1957, he said that he was glad that America was prosperous but that he always had in mind the twenty million Americans who were too poor to maintain even what the rest would call a normal standard of living. In 1958 he was a willing witness in the cases of the release of Nathan Leopold from an Illinois penitentiary and of his early friend Ezra Pound from a Washington mental hospital. He followed John F. Kennedy's Presidential campaign with sympathetic interest. He approved of the Democratic platform, saw in it much that he had seen the Social-Democrats stress in 1908. He was so pleased with Kennedy's inaugural address in January, 1961, that soon after he read all of it before the Daughters of the American Revolution in Republican Orange County, California, pausing frequently to comment, "This is Lincolnesque." [10] In October, 1961, he spoke out sharply in criticism of former President Eisenhower's "easy and careless blast" against the idea of the Peace Corps.[11]

Abraham Lincoln is always his companion. On the centennial of Lincoln's first inauguration, Washington was the scene of a re-enactment of the ceremony. Carl Sandburg spoke. "It was a great day in American history, of which we might say it was the sunset and dawn, moonrise and noon sun, dry leaves in an autumn wind, and springtime blossoms, dying time, birthing hour. And birthing hour." [12] (He repeated it slowly.) Always confident that the people will somehow muster the strength to come through any crisis, he suggested that what was needed in the present hour was the revitalization of the spirit that had been Lincoln's. "Dreamers of deep sacred dreams, finders and welders, sons and daughters of deep burning quests shall come."

IV *Sandburg's Place in Literature*

Responsible critics—as has been noted throughout this book—have been of two minds about Carl Sandburg. For some he is tiresome and unreadable, or even beneath notice. John Crowe Ransom, in making an assessment of American poets between 1900 and 1950—what he called "tentative" judgment—listed as minor poets Vachel Lindsay, William Carlos Williams, Ezra Pound, Marianne Moore, E. E. Cummings, and Hart Crane. He was on the fence about Wallace Stevens. Definitely major in stature were Edwin Arlington Robinson, Robert Frost, and T. S. Eliot. He made no mention at all of Sandburg, whose *Complete Poems* had given the world 676 pages for consideration.[13] Ransom and many of his colleagues and disciples had not found Sandburg's brand of *vers libre* palatable. If he had been a man of promise in 1914, he had failed to develop. As for his prose, according to some critics, it did not meet the standards of imaginative writing often enough to qualify as literature.[14] On the other hand, Sandburg has had his defenders, Gay Wilson Allen and Seymour Krim among them.[15]

One must in the end come to his own conclusion. The criticism of a writer of one's own day must of necessity be partly a matter of individual predilections and partly a matter of fashion. Of a writer as controversial as Sandburg it is not easy to say what of his work is of permanent worth, or if indeed any of it deserves such an accolade.

This book has tried to show Sandburg's weaknesses as well as his strong points. In quick summary, one must admit to diffuseness; fogginess; uninterpreted lists, facts, and anecdotes; prosiness in verse; and irrelevant rhapsodizing in prose. But what else? Has Sandburg contributed anything individual and permanent to American literature?

The answer is yes. At his best he has managed clarity, color, and suggestion—elements effective in both poetry and prose. Emotional energy is evident as well as melodic variety. In the

CARL SANDBURG

Lincoln biography and in *Always the Young Strangers* the simplicity of sentence structure and of paragraph outline and the uncomplicated month-by-month organization of materials compile anecdotes and incidents that eventually give an impressive idea of what Lincoln, his colleagues, and his times were like and of how Galesburg and the surrounding prairie grew gradually more and more meaningful to a son of Swedish immigrant parents.

Of the prose works, *Always the Young Strangers* is unquestionably the best book. A few scattered chapters in *Abraham Lincoln* qualify as excellent, especially, in *The War Years*, the chapters on the "Gettysburg Address," on the assassination, and on the subsequent journey of the body back to Springfield. In both *The Prairie Years* and *The War Years* the character sketches are the work of an artist: for example, Harriet Beecher Stowe, John Brown, and Dred Scott from the first book; and Jefferson Davis, Stanton, Chase, and Seward, Charles Sumner, Thaddeus Stevens, Horace Greeley, and Robert E. Lee from the second. But such paragraphs are only stones from which the whole work is built. The monumental effect of the six volumes is achieved through steady piling up of details—some interesting, some inevitably tedious.

Of the short poems, one begins with "Chicago" and "The Harbor" as representative of the poet's two sides. On the whole, one would select *Chicago Poems* as the best book. It contains no long poem. Except for "Onion Days," "Bath," "Government," "Sheep," and "Silver Nails," all the poems in this book have as much intensity, vision, and skill as Sandburg was to achieve. In the later books, the short poems continue the same vein, though less and less on the vituperative side and more and more on the lyrical. In *Cornhuskers* one would name as the best "Prairie," "Sunset from Omaha Hotel Window," "Band Concert," "Three Pieces on the Smoke of Autumn," "Chicago Poet," "Buffalo Bill," "Interior," "Near Keokuk," all the poems in the section called "Haunts," especially "Cool Tombs," from the section called "Shenandoah" the title poem, "New Feet," "Old Osawatomie," "Grass," "Flanders," "Gargoyle," and "Old Timers." From *Smoke and Steel* one chooses the title poem, "Honky Tonk in Cleveland, Ohio," "Soup," "Blue Island Intersection," "The Hangman at Home," "The Sins of Kalamazoo," "Broken-Face

Gargoyles," "Jazz Fantasia," "Purple Martins," "Four Preludes on Playthings of the Wind," "Bas-Relief," "Bronzes," all the poems in the section called "Mist Forms," "Accomplished Facts," "Chords," all the poems in the sections called "Passports," "Circles of Doors," "Haze," and "Panels."

In *Slabs of the Sunburnt West* the long poem "The Windy City" is best. The title poem is not so intense or authentic, but it deserves preservation for some passages. "Washington Monument by Night" has merit, as have several of the brief impressions: "Black Horizons," "Sea Slant," "Upstream," "At the Gates of Tombs," "Hoof Dusk," "Harsk, Harsk," and "Primer Lesson." The long title poem of *Good Morning, America* begins the cataloguing of folk sayings, but it has enough emotion and movement to warrant citation. The rest of the poems in the book continue the lyric mixture of gentleness and slang. Four of the poems are weaker than the rest, because of either an excess of sentimentality or an annoying prosiness: "Early Lynching," "Epistle," "They Ask: Is God, Too, Lonely?" and the concluding piece, the dull and wordy "Many Hats." The reader can accept almost any of the other poems in the book as representative of the Sandburg idiom.

The People, Yes may be, as Willard Thorp declares, one of the books for the shelf of American classics, yet one cannot name it as absorbingly readable. It is good to refer to for information. Of the lyric tissue that joins the catalogues one selects the following sections as the best: 1, 13, 16, 24, 29, the first part of 35, 75, 77, 87, 103, 106, and the final 107. In *Complete Poems*, of the "New Section" the two best poems are "The Long Shadow of Lincoln: A Litany" and "When Death Came April Twelve 1945."

Nothing in Sandburg's verse equals the best poetry yet written in America—for example, the best of Robinson or Frost, of Wallace Stevens or of William Carlos Williams. But one can say with confidence that to have read Sandburg is to have been in the company of a profoundly sincere American and of a craftsman capable of communicating pity, scorn, brawn, beauty, and an abiding love.

Many readers have put emphasis on Sandburg's humanitarianism, on his defense of the mob—and rightly so. What needs to be stressed finally is his awareness also of the individual's own problems. From early to late, from "The Shovel Man" in *Chicago Poems* through the lonely Lincoln of *The War Years* to even the sunny boy of *Always the Young Strangers*, he showed that not only *man* but *each man* has his troubles and his pleasures, his sorrows and his ecstasies.

Moreover, though the poet's roots are in Illinois, what must be disproved is the impatient and ultimately thoughtless opinion of critical readers who hold that Sandburg has been provincial to a fault, that he has not let himself go in the world of universals. At best this is a specious view. In *Moby Dick* Captain Peleg asks the youthful Ishmael: "Can't ye see the world where you stand?" Thoreau in jail or in a cabin at Walden Pond was no provincial. One can travel far in Concord, in Galesburg, or even in Chicago.

Notes and References

Chapter One

1. For biographical data I have drawn, generally without burdensome documentation, from the New York *Times;* from the brochure published by the University of Illinois for *An Exhibit of Materials from Carl Sandburg's Library: The Sandburg Range, Placed on Display in the University of Illinois Library on January 6, 1958;* and from three books: for the first twenty years, from Carl Sandburg's *Always the Young Strangers* (New York, 1953); through the writing of *The War Years,* from Karl Detzer's *Carl Sandburg* (New York, 1941); for the entire life, from Harry Golden's *Carl Sandburg* (Cleveland and New York, 1961).

2. Lewis Nichols, "Talk with Carl Sandburg," New York *Times Book Review.* January 4, 1953, p. 18.

3. *Complete Poems* (New York: Harcourt, Brace, 1950), p. 176. Hereafter in the text I shall use the abbreviation *CP* and the page number for material quoted from this source.

4. The notebooks, the *Infantry Drill Regulations,* and the dictionary were in the University of Illinois display, 1958; described in *An Exhibit . . . University of Illinois,* pp. 24-25.

5. See note 2.

6. Michael Yatron. *America's Literary Revolt* (New York, 1959), pp. 123-64. Vachel Lindsay and Edgar Lee Masters are the other poets considered.

7. *Philip Green Wright, 1861-1934.* No publication data. The pamphlet is in the Knox College Library. Sandburg's letter is on page 15.

Chapter Two

1. Harriet Monroe, *A Poet's Life* (New York, 1938), p. 322.

2. "New Lamps for Old," *The Dial,* LVI (March 16, 1914), 231-32.

3. Harriet Monroe, "Poetry's Banquet," *Poetry: A Magazine of Verse,* IV (April, 1914), 26-27.

4. Edgar Lee Masters, *Across Spoon River* (New York, 1936), p. 345; Dorothy Dudley, *Forgotten Frontiers: Dreiser and the Land of the Free* (New York, 1932), pp. 415-16.

5. Ben Hecht, *A Child of the Century* (New York, 1954), pp. 244-49.

6. Monroe, *A Poet's Life,* p. 368.

7. Ben Hecht, "Slobberdom, Sneerdom, and Boredom," *The Little Review,* II (June-July, 1915), 25.

8. Masters, *Across Spoon River,* p. 337. •

9. Dudley, *Forgotten Frontiers,* pp. 291, 417-20; F. O. Matthiessen, *Theodore Dreiser* (New York, 1951), p. 218.

10. Golden, *Carl Sandburg,* pp. 65-66.

11. "Chicago Granite," *Poetry: A Magazine of Verse,* VIII (May, 1916), 90-93.

12. "Sonnet" ("Oh for a poet"), *Collected Poems* (New York: Macmillan, 1937), p. 93.

13. William A. Bradley, "Four American Poets," *The Dial,* LXI (December 14, 1916), 528-30. The other three poets were Robert Frost, Amy Lowell, and Edgar Lee Masters. William Stanley Braithwaite's review was in the Boston *Transcript,* May 13, 1916, p. 6.

Chapter Three

1. Hecht, *A Child of the Century,* pp. 249, 252.

2. "Poetry and Verse Technic," *Review of Reviews,* LIX (January 1919), 107; O. W. Firkins, "Pathfinders in America," *The Nation,* CVIII (January 4, 1919), 20-21; Louis Untermeyer, "Strong Timber," *The Dial,* LXV (October 5, 1918), 263-64. *The Dial* was less hostile. Its editors had asked Untermeyer to devote his entire review to the Sandburg book, whereas *Chicago Poems,* two years before, had had to share attention with three other volumes of verse in a single review.

3. "Notes for a Preface," *Complete Poems,* p. xxvi.

4. Eleanor Ruggles, *The West-Going Heart: A Life of Vachel Lindsay* (New York, 1959), p. 261.

Chapter Four

1. Cf. Arthur Wilson, "Sandburg: A Psychiatric Curiosity," *The Dial,* LXX (January, 1921), 80-81; Amy Lowell, "Poetry and Propaganda," New York *Times Book Review,* October 24, 1920, p. 7; "Smoke and Steel," London *Times Literary Supplement,* December 9, 1920, p. 816; William Stanley Braithwaite, Boston *Transcript,* October 16, 1920, p. 7; Louis Untermeyer, "Smoke and Steel," *The New Republic,* XXV (December 15, 1920), 86.

2. Quoted in Golden, *Carl Sandburg,* pp. 177-79.

3. "Carl Sandburg, Human Being," *The Bookman,* LII (January, 1921), 285-90.

4. "Introduction," *Poems by Walt Whitman* (New York, 1921), p. x.

Notes and References

5. Malcolm Cowley, "Two American Poets," *The Dial*, LXXIII (November, 1922), 562-67. The other poet was Conrad Aiken. The other reviews here cited are as follows: Arthur Guiterman, "Chanters and Singers," *The Independent*, CIX (August 5, 1922), 53-54; "Sandburg's Virile Slabs," New York *Times Book Review*, June 4, 1922, p. 11; Harriet Monroe, "His Home Town," *Poetry: A Magazine of Verse*, XX (September, 1922), 332-38.

Chapter Five

1. Edmund Wilson, *Patriotic Gore* (New York, 1962), pp. 115-17.
2. Noting some of these errors were the following reviewers: William E. Barton, *American Historical Review*, XXXI (July, 1926), 809-11; J. A. Woodburn, *American Political Science Review*, XX (August, 1926), 674; "D. R.," *The Independent*, LXVI (February 13, 1926), 193.
3. "Out of the Wilderness," *The Nation and Athenaeum*, XXXIX (May 1, 1926), 130.
4. Wayne Gard, *International Book Review*, IV (February, 1926), 189.
5. July, 29, 1926, p. 503.
6. Cf. Leon Whipple, "Poets Americano," *Survey*, LXI (November 1, 1928), 169; Horace Gregory, "Sandburg's Salutations," *Poetry: A Magazine of Verse*, XXXIII (January, 1929), 214-18; Babette Deutsch, "Seen During a Moment," New York *Herald Tribune Books*, October 21, 1928, p. 2; Mark Van Doren, "The Tender Swede," *The Nation*, CXXVII (October 3, 1928), 76; Percy Hutchinson, "Carl Sandburg Sings Out, 'Good Morning, America,'" New York *Times Book Review*, October 21, 1928, p. 2.

Chapter Six

1. Morton Dauwen Zabel, "Sandburg's Testament," *Poetry: A Magazine of Verse*, XLIX (October, 1936), 33-45. Other reviews include the following: Stephen Vincent Benét, "Carl Sandburg—Poet of the Prairie People," New York *Herald Tribune Books*, August 23, 1936, pp. 1-2; Ben Belitt, "The Majestic People," *The Nation*, CXLIII (1936), 215-16; "Poets and People," *Time*, XXVIII, August 31, 1936, 47; Mildred Boie, *North American Review*, CCXLII (Winter, 1936), 424-27; William Rose Benét, "Memoranda on Americans," *Saturday Review of Literature*, XIV (August 22, 1936), 6.
2. Robert Van Gelder, "His Job Well Done, Sandburg Relaxes," New York *Times*, December 11, 1939, p. 20.
3. Robert Van Gelder, "An Interview with Mr. Carl Sandburg," New York *Times Book Review*, May 31, 1942, p. 2.

4. Cf. J. G. Randall, *American Historical Review*, XLV (July, 1940), 917-22; Allan Nevins, "Abe Lincoln in Washington," *Saturday Review of Literature*, XXI (December 2, 1939), 3, 4ff.; Allan Nevins, "Sandburg as Historian," *Illinois Historical Society Journal*, XLV (1952), 361-72.

Chapter Seven

1. *An Exhibit . . . University of Illinois*, p. 6.
2. New York *Times*, June, 7, 1941, p. 6.
3. Robert Van Gelder, "An Interview with Mr. Carl Sandburg," New York *Times Book Review*, May 31, 1942, p. 2.
4. Ralph Thompson, "Story Teller," New York *Times Book Review*, October 10, 1948, p. 8.
5. Cf. Diana Trilling, "Fiction in Review," *The Nation*, CLXVII (October 30, 1948), 500-1; Perry Miller, "Sandburg and the American Dream," New York *Times Book Review*, October 10, 1948 p. 1.
6. John Farrar, "Carl Sandburg's Masterpiece," *The Bookman*, LXIII (March, 1926), 86.
7. Robert E. Spiller *et al.*, eds. (New York, 1948), pp. 778-86.
8. Robert E. Sherwood, "Carl Sandburg's Ride on a Flimmering Floom," New York *Herald Tribune Books*, November 19, 1950, pp. 1, 26; Henry Commager, "He Sings of America's Plain People," New York *Times Book Review*, November 19, 1950, pp. 1, 40.
9. A. B. Green, "Trade Winds: Boston Arts Festival Award," *Saturday Review*, XXVIII (July 30, 1955), 5.
10. Golden, *Carl Sandburg*, p. 40.
11. New York *Times*, October 26, 1961, p. 37.
12. New York *Times*, March 5, 1961, p. 1.
13. John Crowe Ransom, "The Poetry of 1900-1950," *Kenyon Review*, XIII (Summer, 1951), 445-54.
14. William Carlos Williams in reviewing the *Complete Poems* in *Poetry*, LXXVIII (September, 1951), 345-51, was critical of what he thought was the drifting quality of most of the verse—the lack of controlling form. Kenneth Rexroth, in reviewing *The Sandburg Range* in "Search for Sandburg," *The Nation*, CLXXVI (February 22, 1958), 171-72, made the flat statement that Sandburg did not write literary prose at all and that after 1925 his verse had ceased to contain anything of interest. This dictum would condemn all of *Good Morning, America, The People, Yes,* and the "New Section" of *Complete Poems*.
15. Gay Wilson Allen, "Carl Sandburg: Fire and Smoke," *South Atlantic Quarterly*, LIX (Summer, 1960), 315-31; Seymour Krim, "Voice of America," *Commonwealth*, LXII (June 17, 1955), 283-84.

Selected Bibliography

PRIMARY SOURCES

1. Juvenilia

In Reckless Ecstasy. Galesburg: Asgard Press, 1904.
The Plaint of a Rose. Galesburg: Asgard Press, 1904 (?).
Incidentals. Galesburg: Asgard Press, 1904.
Joseffy, An Appreciation. Galesburg: Asgard Press, 1910.

2. Journalism

You and Your Job. Milwaukee: Social-Democratic Publishing Co.
   1908 (Philadelphia: Socialist Party, 1910).
The Chicago Race Riots, July, 1919. New York: Harcourt, Brace
   and Howe, 1919.
Home Front Memo. New York: Harcourt, Brace, 1943.

3. Poetry

Chicago Poems. New York: Henry Holt, 1916.
Cornhuskers. New York: Henry Holt, 1918. (Reprint with *Chicago Poems: Poems of the Midwest.* Cleveland: World, 1946).
Smoke and Steel. New York: Harcourt, Brace and Howe, 1920.
Slabs of the Sunburnt West. New York: Harcourt, Brace, 1922.
Good Morning, America. New York: Harcourt, Brace, 1928.
The People, Yes. New York: Harcourt, Brace, 1936.
Bronze Wood. San Francisco: Grabhorn Press, 1941.
Six New Poems and a Parable. Lexington: University of Kentucky
   Press, 1961.
Honey and Salt, New York: Harcourt, Brace and World, 1963.

4. Biography

Abraham Lincoln: The Prairie Years. New York: Harcourt, Brace,
   1926 (2 vols.).
Steichen the Photographer. New York: Harcourt, Brace, 1929.
Mary Lincoln, Wife and Widow. New York: Harcourt, Brace,
   1932. (Part II, documents edited by Paul M. Angle.)
Abraham Lincoln: The War Years. New York: Harcourt, Brace,
   1939 (4 vols.).

The Photographs of Abraham Lincoln. New York: Harcourt, Brace, 1944. (With Frederick Hill Meserve.)

Lincoln Collector: The Story of Oliver R. Barrett's Great Private Collection. New York: Harcourt, Brace, 1949. (Reprint: New York: Bonanza Books, 1960.)

Always the Young Strangers. New York: Harcourt, Brace, 1953.

5. Fiction

Remembrance Rock. New York: Harcourt, Brace, 1948.

6. Editions

The American Songbag. New York: Harcourt, Brace, 1927.

A Lincoln and Whitman Miscellany. Chicago: Holiday Press, 1938.

The New American Songbag. New York: Broadcast Music, 1950. (Many new songs.)

7. Collections and Selections

Selected Poems (Rebecca West, ed.). London: Cape, 1926; New York: Harcourt, Brace, 1926.

Storm over the Land: A Profile of the Civil War. New York: Harcourt, Brace, 1942. (From *Abraham Lincoln: The War Years.*)

Complete Poems. New York: Harcourt, Brace, 1950. (With "New Section.")

Abraham Lincoln: The Prairie Years and the War Years. New York: Harcourt, Brace, 1954. (Condensed from six-volume work, with new material.) (Reprint: *Carl Sandburg's Abraham Lincoln,* 3 vols.; New York: Dell, 1960.)

The Sandburg Range. New York: Harcourt, Brace, 1957. (Anthology, with new material.)

Harvest Poems 1910-1960. New York: Harcourt Brace, 1960. (Selection, with "New Poems.")

The World of Carl Sandburg. New York: Harcourt, Brace and World, 1961. ("A Stage Presentation by Norman Corwin." Comments by Sandburg.)

8. Children's Books

Rootabaga Stories. New York: Harcourt, Brace, 1922.

Rootabaga Pigeons. New York: Harcourt, Brace, 1923.

Abe Lincoln Grows Up. New York: Harcourt, Brace, 1928. (First twenty-six chaps. of *Abraham Lincoln: The Prairie Years.*)

Rootabaga Country. New York: Harcourt, Brace, 1929. (Selections.)

Selected Bibliography

Early Moon. New York: Harcourt, Brace, 1930. (Selection of poems.)

Potato Face. New York: Harcourt, Brace, 1930.

Rootabaga Stories. New York: Harcourt, Brace, 1936. (Omnibus.)

Prairie-Town Boy. New York: Harcourt, Brace, 1955. (From *Always the Young Strangers.*)

Wind Song. New York: Harcourt, Brace, 1960. (Selection of poems.)

SECONDARY SOURCES

The following selective list includes biographical and critical materials of use to the student of Sandburg.

ALLEN, CHARLES. "Cadenced Free Verse," *College English,* IX (January, 1948), 195-99. Somewhat technical examination of rhythms in "Nocturne in a Deserted Brickyard" (natural line divisions) and "Chicago" (three major rhythms).

ALLEN, GAY WILSON. "Carl Sandburg: Fire and Smoke," *South Atlantic Quarterly,* LIX (Summer, 1960), 315-31. Discusses Sandburg's considerable sense of structure, though inconsistent control of idea and feeling.

ARVIN, NEWTON. "Carl Sandburg," *New Republic,* LXXXVIII (September 9, 1936), 119-21. Sees slang as clarifier, but also sometimes as "decoy" from full truth. Reprinted in *After the Genteel Tradition,* Malcolm Cowley, ed. (New York: Norton, 1936), pp. 79-87.

BENÉT, STEPHEN VINCENT and ROSEMARY BENÉT. "Sandburg: Son of the Lincoln Countryside," New York *Herald Tribune Books,* December 14, 1941, p. 8. Biographical data and personal relationships.

BRENNER, RICA. *Ten Modern Poets.* New York: Harcourt, Brace, 1930. "Carl Sandburg," pp. 119-48, relates biography to poetry. Two moods: "social and lyrical."

CARGILL, OSCAR. "Carl Sandburg: Crusader and Mystic," *English Journal* (April, 1950), pp. 177-84. Traces Sandburg's development from description of "Chicago" to mystical faith of *The People, Yes.*

COUSINS, NORMAN. "Medicine for the Chicago Anarchists," *Saturday Review of Literature,* XXVI (October 9, 1943), p. 12. Editorial review of *Home Front Memo* as social comment.

DETZER, KARL. *Carl Sandburg: A Study in Personality and Background.* New York: Harcourt, Brace, 1941. Writes of Sandburg as an individual, his methods of working, and the influences of his consummate interest in Lincoln.

DEUTSCH, BABETTE. "Poetry for the People," *English Journal* (College Edition), XXVI (April, 1937), pp. 265-74. Appraisal in the light of Sandburg's desire to communicate with "the average wayfaring man." Though "not so distinguished" as other modern poets, he has different goals.

DUFFEY, BERNARD. *The Chicago Renaissance in American Letters: A Critical History.* East Lansing: Michigan State University Press, 1954. "The Struggle for Affirmation—Anderson, Sandburg, Lindsay," pp. 194-238, develops the thesis that, as Sandburg departs from fact, his ideas are lost in romantic vaporizings.

————. "Progressivism and Personal Revolt," *Centennial Review*, II (Spring, 1958), pp. 125-38. Discusses Garland, Masters, and Sandburg and the Western Populist movement.

GOLDEN, HARRY. *Carl Sandburg.* Cleveland and New York: World, 1961. Anecdotal and intimate, though sometimes inaccurate. Useful for details.

GREGORY, HORACE and MARYA ZATURENSKA. *A History of American Poetry, 1900-1940.* New York: Harcourt, Brace, 1946. "Carl Sandburg," pp. 242-51, ascribes more influence to Lincoln's "Gettysburg Address" than to any other literary source of Sandburg's style.

HANSEN, HARRY. *Midwest Portraits.* New York: Harcourt, Brace, 1923. "Carl Sandburg: Poet of the Streets and of the Prairie," pp. 17-91, describes the poet's Elmhurst workroom, quotes him on his youth, and gives other biographical information.

HOFFMAN, DANIEL G. "Sandburg and 'The People': His Literary Populism Appraised," *Antioch Review*, X (Summer, 1950), pp. 265-78. "In presenting collective emotions divorced from the individual consciousness to a culture as pre-eminently noncollective as ours, Carl Sandburg may have set himself an impossible task." He has lost many otherwise concerned readers.

Illinois Historical Society Journal, XLV (1952), pp. 295-406. Sandburg issue, containing tributes and recollections by Alfred Harcourt, Robert E. Sherwood, Adlai E. Stevenson, Allan Nevins, and many others.

JONES, LLEWELLYN. *First Impressions: Essays on Poetry, Criticism, and Prosody.* New York: Knopf, 1925. "Carl Sandburg: Formalist," pp. 53-68, shows poet's consciously technical use of "quantitative syllable rhythm" and discusses content, satire, and children's stories.

KOLBE, HENRY E. "Christ and Carl Sandburg," *Religion in Life*, XXVII (Spring 1959), pp. 248-61. "Sandburg's Picture of Jesus," "Poems of Wrath and Indignation," "The Eternal Christ."

KRIM, SEYMOUR. "Voice of America," *Commonweal*, LXII (June 17,

1955), pp. 283-84. Review of *Prairie-Town Boy:* "a lean, hard prose that is so whittled to the point that it drives home everything it intends, and yet remains quite boyishly fresh and engaging in spite of its obvious mastery."

LOWELL, AMY. *Tendencies in Modern American Poetry.* Boston: Houghton, Mifflin, 1917. "Edgar Lee Masters and Carl Sandburg," pp. 200-32. Spirited and opinionated commentary. Fears that Sandburg is too much a propagandist.

MONROE, HARRIET. "Carl Sandburg," *Poetry: A Magazine of Verse,* XXIV (September, 1924), pp. 320-26. Great faith in Sandburg. Melodic line beautiful and apt. Reprinted in *Poets and Their Art.* New York: Macmillan, 1926, pp. 29-38.

REXROTH, KENNETH. "Search for Sandburg," *Nation,* CLXXXVI (February 22, 1958), pp. 171-72. A generally angry review of *The Sandburg Range,* violently sure that Sandburg's prose does not qualify as literature.

ROSENFELD, PAUL. *Port of New York: Essays on Fourteen American Moderns.* New York, 1924. "Carl Sandburg," pp. 65-81, is a perceptive early appraisal. Finds it unfortunate that Sandburg "puts blinders on his mind," does not let life have its full way with him. Reprinted from *The Bookman,* LIII (July, 1921), pp. 389-96.

RUBIN, LOUIS D., JR. "Chicago Revisited," *Hopkins Review,* IV (Winter, 1951), pp. 63-69. Review of *Complete Poems,* thorough and sympathetic, bringing balance and justice to earlier reviewers' opinionated myths.

SPILLER, ROBERT E., et al., eds. *Literary History of the United States.* New York: Macmillan, 1948. Willard Thorp's essay on Sandburg, pp. 1181-84, testifies that Sandburg knew America better than Whitman did. "*The People, Yes* is one of the great American books."

STROUD, PARRY. *Carl Sandburg: A Biographical and Critical Study of His Major Works.* Doctoral dissertation: Northwestern, 1956. *Dissertation Abstracts,* XVII, p. 367. Helpful data and interesting analyses.

————. "Sandburg the Young Stranger," *Prairie Schooner,* XXVII (Fall, 1953), pp. 320-28. Main currents in Sandburg's earliest (Galesburg) work.

VAN DOREN, CARL. "Flame and Slag. Carl Sandburg: Poet with Both Fists," *Century,* CVI (September, 1923), pp. 786-92. Urbane discussion of the poet's occasional passion and frequent prosiness, sometimes descending into bathos. Reprinted in *Many Minds.* New York: Knopf, 1942, pp. 136-50.

WEIRICK, BRUCE. *From Whitman to Sandburg.* New York: Macmillan, 1924. Concluding section, pp. 210-21, rates Sandburg as the leader in poetry in the Midwest. A descendant from Whitman, he is a "humanitarian revolutionist."

WEST, REBECCA. "Voice of Chicago," *Saturday Review of Literature,* III (September 4, 1926), pp. 81-83. Is devoted largely to explaining the phenomenon of Chicago to her English audience. Reprinted as her introduction to *Selected Poems of Carl Sandburg.* London: Cape, 1926; New York: Harcourt, Brace, 1926.

WILLIAMS, WILLIAM CARLOS. "Carl Sandburg's *Complete Poems,*" *Poetry: A Magazine of Verse,* LXXVIII (September, 1951), pp. 345-51. Chief criticism: formlessness, a drifting quality. Reprinted in *Selected Essays.* New York: Random House, 1954, pp. 272-79.

WOOD, CLEMENT. *Poets of America.* New York: Dutton, 1925. "Carl Sandburg: A Hymn from Hogwallow," pp. 246-61, takes the stand that *Chicago Poems* was strong, that the succeeding volumes deteriorated.

YATRON, MICHAEL. *America's Literary Revolt.* New York: Philosophical Library, 1959. The influence of Populism on Masters, Lindsay, and Sandburg. Ch. VII, "Carl Sandburg," pp. 123-264, and Ch. VIII, "The Spirit of the Rustic," pp. 165-69, are particularly relevant.

Index

Index